Twayne's Filmmakers Series

Warren French
EDITOR

Robert Altman

Robert Altman directs A Wedding. *Courtesy of Lion's Gate Films, Westwood, CA.*

Robert Altman

GERARD PLECKI

BOSTON

Twayne Publishers

1985

Robert Altman

is first published in 1985 by Twayne Publishers
A Division of G. K. Hall & Company
A publishing subsidiary of ITT
Copyright © 1985 by G. K. Hall & Company
All Rights Reserved

Printed on permanent/durable acid-free paper
and bound in the United States of America

First Printing, 1985

Book Production by Marne B. Sultz

Library of Congress Cataloging in Publication Data

Plecki, Gerard, 1951–
Robert Altman.

(Twayne's filmmakers series)
Bibliography: p. 141
Includes index.
1. Altman, Robert, 1925–   . I. Title.
II. Series.
PN1998.A3A5769   1985   791.43′0233′0924   84-23400
ISBN 0-8057-9303-8

Contents

About the Author

GERARD PLECKI, who was born in Chicago in 1951, received his Ph.D. in English from the University of Illinois at Champaign (1979). Currently a free-lance writer, he has taught film criticism and production for several years at Clemson University and St. Lawrence University. In 1981 he was a NEH Fellow at New York University.

Plecki has written articles on Robert Altman, Hal Ashby, Ken Russell, Jonathan Demme, and contemporary French cinema for various film journals. He is at present completing an original screenplay.

Editor's Foreword

WHEN THIS SERIES OF BOOKS about significant filmmakers was being planned in 1975, Robert Altman was at the peak of his Hollywood career. There was excitement and controversy over his kaleidoscopic epic about America's "Music City," *Nashville*, heightened by the political implications of the film on the eve of our national bicentennial. I particularly wanted to launch this series with a book about Altman, especially when *Nashville* was followed in 1976 by his meditation on American history, *Buffalo Bill and the Indians*, which remains my personal favorite among Altman's films.

An equally enthusiastic friend wanted to take on the assignment, and he appeared the most suitable choice as he had just finished a penetrating study of demonic forces in American literature. Unfortunately, this was also the period when the academic market was drying up; professional problems obliged my friend to abandon the project. Further negotiations with other Altman devotees also broke down because of professional uncertainties that might not allow time for the book.

I then learned from Robert Carringer that a student was finishing a dissertation on Altman at the University of Illinois. I already knew Jerry Plecki through his work as editor of the campus film magazine, *Macguffin;* and when I looked over his study of Altman, I realized that his insights into the often elusive work qualified him as the one who should do the book. What we have here, however, is not simply another published dissertation. Plecki, too, has encountered professional problems that have interfered with the progress of his work; but through difficult years, his own concept of Altman has expanded and matured, and he has carefully rethought, reworked, and greatly tightened his critique, so that within the limit of the series format he has been able to provide a remarkably comprehensive overview of Altman's extensive and varied achievement.

Thus the tribute to Altman that I hoped would lead off this series comes near its end, when the filmmaker's own reputation is vastly different from what it was a decade ago. Indeed, Altman has already quit filmmaking once, although he has returned—for the time being—to low-budget experimental films derived from off-Broadway plays. The days of the great spectacles—*M*A*S*H, Nashville, Buffalo Bill and the Indians, A Wedding, Health, Popeye*—seem to be over; but it is impossible to prophesy about Altman, who is only sixty and may still have surprises in store.

Clearly, however, the sale of the Lion's Gate studio in 1981 after the completion of *Popeye* signaled a major turning point in the director's career. Although best known for his fast-moving episodic films with large casts and multiple plots, a personal favorite among his works has remained the cryptic *Images*, which has also been a favorite of some who have remained most devoted to him. In contrast to the carnival-like extravaganzas, which have captured memorable glimpses from the passing parade with a wry wit and critically bemused eye, *Images* presents the internalized world of a mentally disturbed person. To the publicizing of such private worlds, Altman has returned. Although there is talk about the town and world beyond in *Come Back to the Five and Dime, Jimmy Dean, Jimmy Dean*, outside Woolworth's viewers see only mists. The characters are trapped in the dying world of twenty years before, when James Dean and George Stevens's *Giant* company brought the town its brief day in the sun. *Jimmy Dean* won the grand prize at the Chicago Film Festival in 1982, but it has had only limited distribution through art theaters and college film series, many of which exist precariously with no firm prospects for continuing support. The general public has not taken to Altman's films that critics have admired; and the two that have been most popular with the public—*M*A*S*H* and *Popeye*—have received mixed professional reviews and are among the few projects that Altman himself did not originate and that he was not the first choice to direct. His work—like many distinguished films from abroad and the experiments of some young Americans—requires small, comfortable theaters with the excellent technical equipment that shopping-center cinemas lack. It remains to be seen, however, whether there is any possibility of developing such a fragile subspecies within an American film establishment that cultivates spectacles costing an average of $15 million each.

The best hope would seem to lie in television, whence Altman came to Hollywood. But it seems also most unlikely that American television will develop any equivalent to the British Fourth Program, which has already originated bold experimental works (such as *Moonlighting*) that have been successfully transferred to the big screen. Nothing on American television recently has matched Altman's artistic achievement except for the original BBC "Masterpiece Theater" dramatization of Aldous Huxley's novel *Point, Counterpoint*—another work that is too little known and appreciated.

Despite the problems that he increasingly faces, Altman stands out as the foremost experimenter in broadening the scope and intensifying the concerns of the motion picture since D. W. Griffith and Charlie Chaplin. Even John Ford, Alfred Hitchcock, and other respected directors maintained their reputation by concentrating on the perfection of a single genre, rather than by taking chances on discovering new possibilities that the screen might offer. Not since Griffith's *Intolerance* has an American filmmaker created, as Altman has in *Nashville*, a twentieth-century equivalent in a visual medium of the panoramic qualities of the nineteenth century's multi-plotted Dickensian novels.

Altman's "communal" method of filmmaking, which Gerard Plecki describes in detail in connection with some of the most ambitious projects—like the filming of *Popeye* in Malta—merits citation in itself as an example of a unique sensibility applied to achieving new effects in cinema. Clearly communal sharing and improvisational filmmaking are not suited for all players or projects; but this kind of experimentation is needed if film is to continue to realize the infinite variety and quality of which it is capable. Although Altman's work has been uneven, it has never been trite or predictable. Since this aspect alone evidences rare genius, he cannot be ignored in any study of American cinema as an art. Let us hope that we have not seen the last of his ventures and that those he has already made may become more readily available to those interested in film's permanently valuable repertoire. (At this writing only *M*A*S*H*, *McCabe and Mrs. Miller*, *Nashville*, and *Popeye* are available on commercial videotapes.)

In this book, Gerard Plecki has properly concentrated on the uniqueness of Robert Altman's approach to filmmaking, and often underappreciated accomplishments, in a concise and lively manner that we hope may help the director attract the new audiences that his work merits.

W. F.

Preface

ROBERT ALTMAN HAS BEEN in love with cinema and the magical qualities of film for most of his life. His films demonstrate the lengths to which he will go to capture that magic, that release into a different world, for his viewers. Altman desperately wants viewers to recognize that both fiction and reality can be more exciting than routines and traditions indicate. The only way Altman can achieve this end is to create a world of nonconformity, where characters act unpredictably and violate the expectations of their culture. There is a tendency in his work to "overreach" his material. Altman wants to overwhelm viewers, to move them beyond the confines of theater and screen—not bore them with mundane or extraneous details. There are consequent problems with this approach: gaps in the narrative, or leaps of logic in the development of a theme. These qualities are challenges that, paradoxically, disturb some viewers and delight others.

Altman films are difficult, but never condescending or pretentious. Even casual viewers can discern immediately an air of honesty, spontaneity, and realism in his films. Altman's techniques are audacious. His greatest film, *Nashville*, stars wholly unknown actors and actresses, all of whom composed their own songs. Altman constantly encourages actors to improvise or to adjust the script. The director generally follows a very innovative production format of evolution, negotiation, and experimentation. He is willing to use hunches and visions to begin and guide his projects. He shoots films in sequence as he develops the narrative line. Altman has even created new sound systems to enliven the dialogue. As his own producer, he has maintained complete artistic integrity in his films.

Robert Altman's credo of freedom, experimentation, and often indulgence is apparent in all of his films. His maverick sensibility is, invariably, infuriating to some of the critics all of the time. Some of his films are weak because they are too ambiguous (*Brewster McCloud* and *Quintet*). Other films (*Nashville* and *Buffalo Bill*) are best when they are ambiguous. Each film is elusive and enigmatic.

Within each film, Altman suggests that more is happening to the characters than may be apparent at any given time. Throughout each film, Altman presses the viewer to accept a new set of rules. By following his advice to "giggle and give in" to the on-screen universe, it is possible for the viewer to appreciate the poetic expressions—of life's traumas, rewards, contradictions, and pleasures—that abound in the films of Robert Altman.

The publication of this book would not have been possible without the help and support of my parents and entire family. I am indebted to Robert Carringer and Susan Brown for their editorial assistance. I would also like to thank Warren French, Kathleen McCarthy, and Thomas Ryan for their support and advice. Finally, although my father passed away before this book was completed, his influence has been felt and appreciated.

GERARD PLECKI

Chronology

1925	Robert Altman born in Kansas City, Missouri, February 20.
1943	Enters the army and serves as a bombardier in fifty missions over Borneo and the Dutch East Indies.
1947	Discharged from the army. Marries Lavonne Elmer. Attends the University of Missouri for a year. Coauthors *Christmas Eve* with Edwin Marin.
1948	Writes *The Bodyguard* with George W. George for a film by Richard Fleischer.
1949	Moves to New York City to write scripts, then goes to Hollywood with Lou Lombardo in an unsuccessful attempt to sell several scripts. Gets first divorce.
1950	Returns to Kansas City and produces a series of documentaries for the Calvin Company and International Harvester. Marries Lotus Corelli.
1955	Directs first film, *The Delinquents* (not released until 1957). Gets second divorce.
1957	*The James Dean Story* (codirected with George W. George). Marries present wife, Kathryn. Moves to Hollywood and directs episodes for various television shows.
1963	Forms Lion's Gate Films with Ray Wagner in Westwood (Los Angeles). Develops a scenario for *Petulia* with Wagner, then drops the project.
1964	*Nightmare in Chicago*. Abandons television career and begins a long period of unemployment.
1966	*Countdown* (released in 1968).
1969	*That Cold Day in the Park.*
1970	*M*A*S*H. Brewster McCloud.*
1971	*McCabe and Mrs. Miller.*

1972   *Images.*

1973   *The Long Goodbye.*

1974   *Thieves Like Us. California Split.*

1975   *Nashville.*

1976   *Buffalo Bill and the Indians, Or, Sitting Bull's History Lesson.* Fired from *Ragtime.*

1977   *Three Women.* Produces *Welcome to L.A.* and *The Late Show.*

1978   *A Wedding.* Produces *Remember My Name.*

1979   *Quintet. A Perfect Couple.* Produces *Rich Kids.* Expands Lion's Gate, naming Tommy Thompson president and Robert Eggenweiler vice-president.

1980   *Health. Popeye.*

1981   Fired from *Lone Star.* Announces the end of his commercial filmmaking. Directs one-act plays in Los Angeles and off-Broadway.

1982   *Come Back to the Five and Dime, Jimmy Dean, Jimmy Dean* (prior to its release, directs *Jimmy Dean* on Broadway.)

1983   *Streamers* premieres at the New York Film Festival.

1984   *Secret Honor.*

1

The Early Years

THE CHARACTERS IN THE FILM WORLD of Robert Altman have at least one shared trait—their unpredictability. They act on impulses. They undermine cultural norms and flaunt social conventions. Hawkeye and Trapper (*M*A*S*H*) operate in a hospital on the Korean front, but they act as though they are at an Ivy League fraternity reunion. Brewster McCloud believes he is Dedalus; so one day he jumps off a balcony inside the Houston Astrodome in a "flying" escape from police pursuit. Cathryn (*Images*) kills her husband because she thinks he is a hallucination. The characters often seem to be following some obscure plan all their own.

The life of Robert Altman has certainly been unpredictable, but there is a hazy autobiographical pattern evident in his choice of subject matter for films. He was born in 1925 in Kansas City and raised as a Catholic. Religion never affected his life very much—but still Altman states he based a film (*Images*) on a poem he wrote about a Jesuit school he had attended. Gambling was a large influence for his adolescence. His father was a gambler, and Altman recalled, "I learned a lot about losing from him."[1] His ambivalence toward the phenomenon of gambling surfaces in *California Split*. At the age of eighteen he entered the army and flew fifty missions as a bombardier over the East Indies. Upon his release in 1948 he forgot about military service and took odd jobs. The oddest was tattooing identification numbers on dogs. It was not until twenty years later, however, that he exorcised his feelings about the military in *M*A*S*H*.

Altman thus had a long "gestation period," much lengthier than that of Truffaut, Scorsese, Bogdanovich, or Lucas, who were raised on film. Altman once commented, "I never knew there was a movie director"[2] until he saw David Lean's *Brief Encounter*. Then a fascination with film took over his life. He began writing scripts and studying international cinema. He wrote *The Bodyguard*, which he sold in Hollywood. This success encouraged him to spend a year in New York City, writing plays and novels. Unfortunately, his tenure in New York did not produce any offers.

And so, around 1950, Altman decided to return to Kansas City, and to begin some serious work in film production. He found a job at the Calvin

Robert Altman with Warren Beatty on location for McCabe and Mrs. Miller. *Courtesy of Warner Bros., Burbank, CA.*

Company, where he learned many aspects of documentary film production. He designed sets, operated cameras, began directing industrial films, and eventually produced a series of short technical films for International Harvester.

— After three or four years of this sort of apprenticeship, Altman was eager to venture into commercial filmmaking on his own. So in the summer of 1955 he began work on *The Delinquents*. He wrote the script in five days and borrowed $63,000 to shoot it on location in his hometown. He must have been influenced by *The Blackboard Jungle* (1955) because he cast Peter Miller from that film and Tom Laughlin (*Billy Jack*, 1971) as the leads. For the rest of the cast, he used thirteen local actors and actresses, including his second wife (Lotus Corelli) and his daughter.

In its seventy-one minutes, *The Delinquents* tells the story of a teenage couple who love each other in spite of parental objections. Scotty (Tom Laughlin) plans to go out with Janice (Rosemary Howard) with the help of his juvenile-delinquent friends. When the police raid their party and arrest several gang members, the hoods blame Scotty, kidnap him, and abandon him at the scene of a murder to "take the fall." After several fights Scotty frees his abducted girlfriend and reports to the police the activities and whereabouts of the gang.

The stereotypic setting, melodramatic exchanges, and simplistic love story qualify *The Delinquents* as an exploitative "teenage hoodlum" formula film. Altman moved the *film noir* violence and rebellion of the early 1950s (e.g., *The Big Heat*) from urban ghettoes to the suburbs. He incorporated aspects of the "troubled youth" films that had been released just prior to the making of *The Delinquents*, such as drinking and rebellion in Kramer's *The Wild One* (1954). The film also featured a voice-over narration that the director claimed was added after the sale of the film. For a $150,000 investment United Artists received a cheap "troubled teen" film that, upon its release in March 1957, grossed a million dollars from a brief, secondary market distribution.

In *Kings of the Bs*, Todd McCarthy argues that *The Delinquents* was the precursor of many Altman films, sharing elements found in *McCabe and Mrs. Miller*, *Thieves Like Us*, and *The Long Goodbye*. In actuality the themes and techniques have very little in common with later Altman films. *The Delinquents* makes a clichéd appeal to community groups to "stop this spread of violence," but the culture is not blamed for the erratic actions of its youths. In other Altman films such as *McCabe and Mrs. Miller* and *Thieves Like Us* the actions of the outlaws reflect the hypocritical and selfish attitudes condoned and practiced by society. The characters in *Brewster McCloud* and *Thieves Like Us* are rebels, as they are in *The Delinquents*. Unlike *The Delinquents*, however, Altman's later social rebels are complex, humorous, and often heroic individuals.

Although *The Delinquents* is not impressive cinema, it was a challenge for Altman. It introduced him to the mechanics of feature film production; it also convinced him never to work with Tom Laughlin again. Although it was an interesting first outing, the director's summation of the film is probably quite accurate: "Nobody knew what they were doing. I don't think it has any meaning for anybody."[3]

After the death of James Dean in 1955, Altman and his friend and collaborator George W. George pieced together *The James Dean Story*. This was a pseudodocumentary compilation film containing a voice-over narration, still photographs, screen tests, and movie clips of the late actor. It pretended to investigate the "mystery" of the star. The film, running nine minutes longer than *The Delinquents*, was released in 1957 by Warner Brothers and met with dismal critical and box-office reception.

George W. George is often cited as sole director of the film, but it was an equally disastrous venture for Altman, who would approach the topic again in 1982 in his much more successful film, *Come Back to the Five and Dime, Jimmy Dean, Jimmy Dean*. In any case, had *The James Dean Story* been immediately released in 1955, it most likely would have returned a profit. Instead, after it was quickly assembled, it was then withheld by Warner Brothers for one and a half years. While there was a staunch group of Dean followers who would consume any Dean *hommage*, it was not clear to Warner Brothers that the film would have any appeal. In the end even Dean fans in 1957 did not appreciate this superficial elegy by Altman and George.

The two men chose several unfortunate strategies for *The James Dean Story* that especially annoyed Dean fanatics. Their first mistake was to rely on a narration, read by Martin Gabel, which was no more than a series of unrelated rhetorical questions and guarded postulations, read in an emotionless manner. The directors raided scrapbooks and indiscriminately used still photographs of Dean, often emphasizing the mangled corpse and his crushed car. Numerous transitional shots of the ocean and beaches were inserted in a random manner. To make matters worse, the directors used an obvious stand-in for Dean, photographed from a distance, to add to the intended realism of the exposé.

A major misapprehension in the film involved the directors' apparent belief that Dean's life was ill-fated because society had condemned him as a troublemaker. They avoided the more complicated thesis that Dean was struggling desperately to understand his place in the world, and failing. *The James Dean Story* thus shared the worst elements of *The Delinquents*: an exploitative nature, insubstantial thematic argument, and a wooden narration.

These two films nevertheless qualified Altman as a commercial director. After the release of *The James Dean Story*, he was hired by Alfred Hitchcock to direct episodes of "Alfred Hitchcock Presents" for CBS. Altman chose to direct two episodes of the series, "The Young One" and "Together," in 1957 and 1958.

Television Years

In the seven years Robert Altman worked in television, from 1957 to 64, he directed more action-adventure shows, romances, westerns, and series pilot shows than did any film directors who began careers in television, including Sidney Lumet, John Frankenheimer, Arthur Penn, and Franklin Schaffner. He worked on at least twenty different shows, including "Combat," "The Detective," "The Millionaire," "Bus Stop," "The Whirlybirds," and "The Roaring Twenties." This work gave Altman a good understanding of the parameters of film genres. Also his experience in television refined his technical abilities. He learned to work quickly and efficiently and to make the most of limited budgets and tight shooting schedules. He developed valuable alliances within the industry. For example, his producer on "East Side, West Side," David Suskind, was his executive producer for *Buffalo Bill and the Indians*. Despite these contacts, he never became an "insider"—he regarded the process of directing television shows as "guerilla warfare . . . how to say things without saying them." He maintained very warm relationships with most cast and crew members and struggled against the institutionalized type-casting of actors. He also began to incorporate suggestive sexual and political themes in his episodes and began using a form of overlapping dialogue similar to that of Hawks and Welles. Understandably, this "warfare" was not without its repercussions. Many producers and sponsors believed that his ideas and techniques, which might shock or confuse viewers, were fairly incompatible with the goal of selling a clearly defined product to the largest possible audience. Altman was, therefore, often fired, but with each job he learned more details for directing. Since the industry was expanding, there was usually a similar production team looking for an experienced director. In each of his jobs throughout this period, the director insisted on his "own personal message throughout the veneer."[4] His nonconformist attitude sometimes caused him some problems. He refused to direct the third script he was given for "Alfred Hitchcock Presents"; he was fired when one of his episodes of "Bus Stop" was deemed "too violent" for public consumption. His tactics were very often audacious. He directed the only antiwar episode in the history of "Combat," a show whose popularity depended on its celebration of the grisly triumphs of an American infantry platoon in France and Germany during World War II. He attacked the strict morality promulgated by John B. Tipton in "The Millionaire" by directing a "really erotic" episode. In each of these cases, Altman reversed general audience expectations for the shows. This procedure foreshadows

Altman's approach to *M*A*S*H*, where he first led the audience to accept war as fun and games, and then caught the audience laughing at a "morally offensive"[5] joke.

Stints with "The Kraft Mystery Theater" and "The Kraft Suspense Theater," whose plots were for Altman "as bland as their cheese,"[6] and, for a long period, with "Bonanza," one of the few shows from which he was not fired, proved significant to his film career. First, Altman directed an episode of "The Kraft Suspense Theater" entitled "Once Upon a Savage Night," which ran for fifty-four minutes and was aired on 2 April 1964. The episode was based on the William P. McGivern novel *Killer on the Turnpike* and it showed police efforts to hunt an escaped convict. Later in the year an expanded version (81 minutes) was released for commercial distribution as *Nightmare in Chicago*, with Altman receiving directorial credit. The film starred Ted Knight as a reporter helping state police to capture the escaped murderer Georgie Porgie (Charles McGraw), who was at large on the Illinois tollway system outside Chicago. Altman used on-location shots and close-ups of the killer's face through the windshield to communicate and maintain a sense of monomania. *Nightmare in Chicago* provided additional recognition for Altman; it also acquainted him with a location he would use for a car-crash scene in a later film of his, *A Wedding*.

Altman's work on "Bonanza" had a broad influence on his artistic development. The themes he investigated and the people he met on this series helped form a basis for several of his later works. Altman has often stated that, while working on one film project, he realized that he had been aware of general concept, plot, or theme for many years. The eight segments of "Bonanza" he directed from 1 September 1960, to 29 June 1961, hint at the first inspirations for films Altman would direct up to ten years later. Several of the episodes changed the structure of the series.

His first episode of "Bonanza," aired on 20 October, was entitled "Silent Thunder." The show narrates the reunion of a man with his deaf daughter. By telling this tale from Little Joe Cartwright's perspective, and avoiding any "miracle cure," the director was able to downplay the sentimental and overtly emotional aspects of the story. The father-daughter reconciliation was a learning experience for the viewer, rather than a simple western "tear-jerker." "Bonanza" episodes in the two years following "Silent Thunder" indicate that the episode precipitated the shift of the series to a ritualistic, morality-play format. The episode, like *That Cold Day in the Park* and *Images*, featured a psychologically tormented female protagonist whose fragile emotional and mental states are symbolically represented by the cluttered props on the set.

After his "Bank Run" episode (documented in the chapter on *McCabe and Mrs. Miller*) and before "The Dream Riders" (mentioned in the *Brewster McCloud* chapter), Altman directed four other episodes of "Bonanza." He made "The Duke," which William R. Cox adapted from the characters of the King and the Duke in *The Adventures of Huckleberry Finn*. The episode told the story of a con artist and a prize fighter who visit Virginia City and challenge Hoss to a boxing exhibition. "The Duke" revealed Altman's love for rogues and gamblers; this fascination with con games is especially evident in *The Long Goodbye, California Split*, and *Nashville*. The episode also brought out the director's warm relationship with Dan Blocker, the starring Cartwright in most of the Altman segments. Through the course of his association with "Bonanza" Altman became a close friend with Blocker. In 1972 he cast Blocker for the role of Roger Wade in *The Long Goodbye*. Blocker's death led Altman to dedicate the film to his memory.

Altman next directed "Sam Hill," retitled "The Mustang." Although its script is absent from the "Bonanza" production files, it is evident from the master shooting schedule and the daily production reports that the show included an inordinately large number of props and guest stars, including Claude Akins and Edgar Buchanan. This episode and "The Rival," shot from 20 to 27 January and aired five weeks later, contained a thematic concern with the nature of prejudice. After a lynching in "The Rival," for example, Hoss comments, "I reckon a man's feelings just don't change overnight," an emotional insight that was a significant one for the strong, silent Cartwright family. Also, "The Secret," filmed from 23 February to 1 March and aired the week after "The Rival," demonstrates Altman's talent for working with large casts and crews. "The Secret" also narrated several stories at once.

His penchant for simultaneous modes of expression continued in his final "Bonanza" episode and became one of his trademarks. "The Many Faces of Gideon Flinch," shot from 22 to 29 July, was prestigiously aired as the last show of the season for "Bonanza." It involved two main plots: Little Joe and Hoss's fascination with a stranger in town named Jennifer, who is shown to be a pickpocket; and the mysterious presence of another newcomer, known interchangeably as Jake and Gideon Flinch. Altman would return to this concept of progressively confused identities in *Images*.

Another tangible benefit from Altman's "Bonanza" experience was his close relationship with producer Tommy Thompson, with whom Altman worked from 1958 to 1963 on "The Troubleshooters," "The Whirlybirds," "Sheriff of Cochise," and other productions. Thompson later served as assistant director on most Altman films, and executive producer on many of them.

By 1964 Altman had endured all the restrictions and the pressures of the television industry that he could countenance. Facing the possibility of spending his life directing mediocre television shows, with a corresponding loss of opportunity for creative expression, he decided to abandon the guerrilla warfare.

The medium had provided Altman with a variety of techniques and ideas; his television career also was a remarkably prolific time for the director. By necessity Altman learned to move quickly from one show to the next. Similarly in the nine-year period from 1960 to 1978 he then directed thirteen films, far more than most contemporary American directors. (In the same period he also produced four other projects through Lion's Gate Films.)

In 1966 he accepted an offer from Warner Brothers to direct a low-budget science-fiction film called *Countdown*, dealing with astronaut Lee Stegler's trip to the moon. (The role of Stegler was played by James Caan.) The preparation for the trip was complicated by rivalries among Lee and his colleagues. Flaring tempers, alcoholism, jealousies, and numerous individual obsessions plague the astronauts, their wives, and the space-program officials.

Selected as the ideal candidate for the job and shoved into a rocket after a brief training period, Lee floats aimlessly through space for a while. Then, when he crashes his ship on the moon and stakes his claim, he discovers another disabled spacecraft, the remains of a Russian expedition. The film ends with Lee waiting in the wreckage, signaling for a rescue ship to be sent from earth.

There are two possible reasons for the artistic and commercial difficulties in *Countdown*. It is possible that Altman was relatively unfamiliar with a genre that he was attempting to change. It is equally likely, however, that *Countdown* could have been an unusual but effective science-fiction film if not for the rebellion of producers William Conrad and Jack Warner. Altman was fired from *Countdown* after the shooting was completed. Viewing the footage, Warner was appalled by the length and decided that a total of thirty minutes should be cut from the film. This deletion included all scenes where two or more actors were simultaneously audible on the soundtrack. Warner also hoped to shift the film from an unsettling character analysis to a more plausible narration of the conquest of space. Warner, of course, eliminated the most interesting concept of the film, that is, the guilt-ridden and anxiety-laden natures of the astronauts, and replaced that concept with standard science-fiction fare of the 1960s.

Still, Lee and Chiv (Robert Duvall) are complex characters. They are unable to separate their professional tasks from their troubled personal lives. They view the project not as a noble scientific venture, but as an escape from relationships that they cannot control. Although that theme is unusual for such a film, it is consistent with the themes in *Brewster McCloud, Thieves Like Us,* and *Quintet,* where the sole destiny of a character seems to be to destroy a system within which he finds himself placed.

That Cold Day in the Park

In 1968 Altman began filming *That Cold Day in the Park*, which was released by Commonwealth United Enterprises in 1969–one month before *M*A*S*H*. Based on a screenplay by Gillian Freeman from a novel by Gerald Perreau Saussine, the film describes the strong attraction of Frances (Sandy Dennis) to a young man (Michael Burns). She sees him sitting in a park in the rain and invites him into her apartment, allowing him to spend the night there. She acts as guardian and provider to the man, who refuses to speak to her. She also desires him as a lover.

Hoping to become intimately involved with the man, she visits a gynecologist and obtains a diaphragm. She is too insecure to initiate an affair, but her desires soon become an obsession. She procures a prostitute for the young man, who by now has comfortably settled into her apartment and has even entertained his sister there, without Frances's knowledge. She introduces him to the prostitute, but a few minutes later she stabs the woman. Frances then reassures the terrified young man that she will protect him, thus control him, in some unexplained, convoluted relationship.

There is more exploitation than artistry in *That Cold Day in the Park*; the casual treatment of frigidity, incest, and prostitution is prurient and sensational, with no apparent "lesson" to be learned. Frances is frustrated and frightened in the film, but the causes of her instability and of her sudden schizophrenic outburst are not suggested. The motivation of the young man poses similar problems of implausibility. The actions of both characters fluctuate unpredictably throughout the film.

That Cold Day is often shocking, but still the viewer does not care very much about the vague problems and insecurities of the two characters. Sandy Dennis is effective in communicating the hesitancy and desperateness of Frances, while Michael Burns's overacting makes the queer movements and strategies of the young man laughable.

Although *That Cold Day* is not a particularly memorable film in itself, one does notice emergent directorial trademarks and style in it. For example, Altman fills each frame with windows, partitions, closets, glass, and chrome. The use of these objects of reflection and isolation is uncontrolled in this film, whereas in *Images* the objects become meticulous and appropriate representations of the protagonist's divided personality and her confused perception of reality.

For *That Cold Day in the Park*, Altman also assembled a technical crew, including Robert Eggenweiler, Leon Erickson, and Graeme Clifford, that worked with him on many later films. The on-location shooting also supplied Altman with information about the Vancouver area and the facilities he could use for *McCabe and Mrs. Miller.* The actors with whom he worked on this film and throughout his television career, including Sandy Dennis, Robert Duvall, Michael Murphy, Barbara Baxley, and others, would star in his later films. More importantly, however, the fact that he was working on commercial films earned the director a modicum of recognition in Hollywood. The attention led directly to his involvement with *M*A*S*H.*

2

*M*A*S*H*

THE PLANS FOR FILMING *M*A*S*H* began early in 1969, when Ingo Preminger, Otto's brother, received a draft of Ring Lardner, Jr.'s screenplay for an antiwar comedy called *M*A*S*H*, based on the 1968 novel by Richard Hooker. Preminger, Richard Zanuck, and Twentieth Century–Fox then compiled a list of possible directors for *M*A*S*H*. Sensing that this could be a lucrative property if the controversial subject matter and language were handled properly, they tended to ignore older, traditional directors such as Fred Zinnemann, Joseph Mankiewicz, or David Lean, and opted for someone like Arthur Penn, Mike Nichols, or Stanley Kubrick, who would be able to attract stars and insure a large box-office draw. Penn, Nichols, and Kubrick were, however, already engaging major stars in projects of their own *(Little Big Man, Catch-22,* and *A Clockwork Orange).* Franklin Schaffner was directing George C. Scott in *Patton* for Fox at the time, George Roy Hill had Paul Newman occupied with *Butch Cassidy and the Sundance Kid,* and Bob Rafelson was filming *Five Easy Pieces* with Jack Nicholson. A dozen other directors who were offered only a director's fee for *M*A*S*H* flatly refused the screenplay.

So with at least seventeen directors either unwilling or unavailable, Preminger approached Altman with the screenplay. In the book *American Film Now* Robert Monaco mentions that Preminger said that if he had seen *That Cold Day in the Park* he would not have hired Altman. Monaco observes that "nothing in Altman's previous checkered career suggested he would do very well with satirical comedy,"[1] which is accurate except for the penchant for tongue-in-cheek treatments noted in Altman's television career. In any case, the director accepted, in spite of initial hesitations, because he "saw in it the opportunity to do something I had been working on for about five years, which was a World War II farce." He had been unable to secure financing for a production of the Roald Dahl short story "Death Where is Thy Sting," and he needed to make a major film very badly after *That Cold Day.* So Zanuck, Preminger, and Altman tried to settle on a strategy for casting the film. Altman related that "we first agreed that we didn't want movie stars, we wanted the personality of the

11

Elliott Gould, Donald Sutherland, and Tim Brown as
M*A*S*H merrymakers. Courtesy of Films Incorporated,
Wilmette, IL.

whole group," which indicated the major influence that Altman already was having on the project.[2]

Like Elliott Gould and Robert Duvall, Donald Sutherland had appeared in films before *M*A*S*H* without winning much recognition. The majority of the cast, however, were introduced to acting in *M*A*S*H*. It was also the director's first "community experience" film. Actors lived in tents set up on the Fox back lot where the film was shot. They developed close relationships with each other and were encouraged to adjust, invent, or delete dialogue from the script during rehearsal periods. Altman was so comfortable with their performances and abilities that he used many of them, including Tom Skerritt, René Auberjonois, Roger Bowen, David Arkin, John Schuck, Michael Murphy, Bud Cort, Tim Brown, G. Wood, Corey Fischer, and of course Elliott Gould in many subsequent films.

Story Line

M*A*S*H is probably Robert Altman's funniest film, even though the quality and type of humor are inconsistent. Often in this film the director pushes a joke too far, as in the shower-scene discussion about the dentist, Walt "Painless Pole" Waldowski (John Schuck). On occasions the use of slapstick is overdone, particularly in the opening fight between the black sergeant and the military police, or in the football game. But for the most part, humor in the film is quick, witty, offhand, and completely realistic. One of Altman's goals along these lines seems to be to unsettle the viewer, that is, after getting a laugh, to force a recognition that the joke is possibly not as funny as it may immediately seem.

These attempts to disorient viewers are evident throughout the episodic film. In the opening credits sequence, the sight of the helicopters (without any live sound) leaving the front lines, along with the calming melody of "Suicide Is Painless," is captivating and poetic, while the lyrics of the theme song warn of the seriousness of the scene. So as soon as we begin to enjoy the dreamy visuals and lullaby, we are told "the sword of time will pierce our skin, it never hurts when it begins"; "the game of life is hard to play, I'm gonna lose it anyway"; and "I can take or leave it if I please," a sentiment that recurs throughout Altman's films especially in "It Don't Worry Me" from *Nashville*.

The film actually does not have any conventional plot. The story, with its series of disjointed episodes, approaches the traditions of the picaresque novel, although the characters here are doctors and officers, rather than vagabond rogues. With the arrival of two of the doctors, Hawkeye Pierce (Donald Sutherland) and Duke Forrest (Tom Skerritt), at the beginning of the film, it is obvious that much of the humor will derive from the attempts of the surgeons to establish themselves as renegades—from their constant struggles to disassociate themselves from army protocol and regulations at every possible opportunity. They quickly assert their independence by ignoring military ranks. Forrest believes that Hawkeye is his driver and tells him to get his bags—he does not discover that Hawkeye is a captain until they meet Lt. Dish (Jo Ann Pflug) and Colonel Henry Blake (Roger Bowen). The atmosphere of the camp is relaxed and informal. Everyone is on a first-name basis; a captain wears private fatigues and tennis shoes, and the conversation in the operating room is strikingly blunt and familiar. At one point in an operation Duke comments, "Man, it looks like the Mississippi River down there" as he operates on the stomach of a patient. When he later needs assistance in an operation, he commandeers the service of the chaplain, Father "Dago Red" Mulcahy (René Auberjonois), who is performing Last Rites on a patient, by telling him, "Sorry, but this man's still alive and that one's dead, and that's a fact."

In addition to the problem of being understaffed, Hawkeye and Duke must live and work with the first of the two "regular army clowns" they meet in the camp, Major Frank Burns (Robert Duvall). They discover that Burns is not only a hypocrite and a religious fanatic but is also an incompetent surgeon. They bully Colonel Blake into moving Burns from their tent and demand that he find a chest surgeon. The arrival of the anonymous surgeon provides a very humorous, small moment in the film. Hawkeye seems to recognize the man, and tells him in a slight western drawl, "I don't know your name, stranger, but your face is familiar." They offer the man a martini, to which he agrees, and then tops their offer by asking, "Don't you use olives?" His initiation to their circle is completed when, to their amazement, he removes a jar of olives from his coatpocket, saying, "Yes, but a man can't really savor a martini without an olive, otherwise it just doesn't quite make it." His alliance with Hawkeye and Duke is reaffirmed when he confronts Burns and punches him in the head, after he had seen Burns blaming the orderly Boone (Bud Cort) for the death of a patient.

While the surgeons are playing football, Hawkeye recalls the identity of the newcomer, Captain "Trapper John" McIntyre (Elliott Gould). The team is now complete, and immediately the antics of the threesome escalate, particularly with the entrance of the new head nurse, Major Houlihan (Sally Kellerman). Hawkeye is at first attracted to her and is friendly, but when he asks where she is from and she replies, "Well, I like to think of the Army as my home," he is warned that he is encountering an alien perspective. The pace and humor of their conversation in the mess tent heighten when Hawkeye states, "If you have observed anything you would have observed that Major Burns is an idiot." Houlihan feels to the contrary, that "Major Burns is not only a good technical surgeon, he is also

a good military surgeon." Hawkeye is stunned; Houlihan is just warming
to her topic. She has also observed that everyone refers to Pierce as
Hawkeye, and "that kind of informality is inconsistent with maximum efficiency in a military organization." By now Hawkeye's patience has been
worn too thin. He tells her, "Oh come off it, Major! You put me right off
my fresh fried lobster, do you realize that?" Hawkeye is not just angry with
her; he is fed up with the control that the army has exerted over everyone's life, including his own. So, understandably, he describes how he
would "normally" have acted and why her remarks have upset him. He
relates that "under normal circumstances, you being normally what I call
a very attractive woman, I would have invited you back to share my little
bed with me and you might possibly have come—but you really put me
off." He therefore concludes that, unfortunately, "you're what we call a
regular army clown." Then when Houlihan asks rhetorically, "I wonder
how a degenerated person like that could have reached a position of authority in the Army Medical Corps," Dago Red casually answers, "He was
drafted." The conversation between the two captains and the reply by
Mulcahy characterize the irony that the surgeons must be experiencing.

Hawkeye's attitude also conveys the anarchic temperament the surgeons adopt in order to adjust to their situation. The tone of the film, and
the actions and attitudes of the surgeons, emulate the style, the behaviors,
and the motivations seen in several Marx Brothers films. The attitude toward war is nearly identical in *M*A*S*H* and *Duck Soup:* Korea is the
same "Land of the Spree and Home of the Knave" for the surgeons that
Freedonia is for Rufus T. Firefly. As far as the army is concerned, the
surgeons seem to agree with the philosophy of Professor Wagstaff, in
Horse Feathers, who sings, "Whatever it is, I'm against it." Hawkeye and
Trapper John alternately show the same sarcasm and lechery that
Groucho Marx displays in countless films. After being named chief surgeon, Trapper dresses in an Uncle Sam outfit while he is carried around
the tent with everyone singing "Hail to the Chief"—a scene reminiscent
of the "Hooray for Captain Spaulding" melee in *Animal Crackers*. Trapper
spots Margaret Houlihan and yells, "No. No food. I want sex. Bring me
some sex. That one there, the sultry bitch with the fire in her eyes. Take
her clothes off and bring her to me." Perhaps his diction is less subtle, but
otherwise there is little difference between his attitude toward Houlihan
in *M*A*S*H* and the approach of Otis B. Driftwood to Mrs. Claypool in
A Night at the Opera—they both intend to use and then discard those
women.

Meanwhile, Altman portrays Burns as a total hypocrite. For example,
he and Margaret complain how those activities are bad for "army morale."
Margaret sympathizes, saying, "It's the disrespect for you, that's what I
can't forgive them." Bent on self-destruction, Frank Burns replies with

Hawkeye (Donald Sutherland) and Trapper John (Elliott Gould) tee off into the battle zone in M*A*S*H. *Courtesy of Aspen/20th Century Fox, Los Angeles, CA.*

unintended irony, "Oh, I'm used to it." Apparently this is not the first time he has earned disrespectful treatment from a bunch of "godless buffoons," one of whom is Radar O'Reilly (Gary Burghoff), the quiet, resourceful company clerk. With his help the surgeons lead an attack on the pretensions they find displayed in abundance in the personalities of Frank and Margaret. For example, Frank and "Hot Lips" need to justify their sexual attraction for each other. Frank suggests, "God meant us to find each other," to which Margaret responds, while throwing open her blouse, "His Will be done." Earlier, on the other hand, when Hawkeye is going to bed with Lieutenant Dish, she just states, "I love my husband," to which Hawkeye truthfully explains, "I love my wife too. If she was here I'd be with her," and "Love has nothing to do with this." His philosophy makes the rationalization of Margaret and Frank appear even more sacrilegious.

Obviously, then, the viewer knows exactly who is going to come out ahead in the Burns and Hawkeye conflict. Over breakfast Hawkeye teases and baits Burns about his brief affair with Hot Lips, asking him, "Heard from your wife lately?" and "Is she better than self-abuse?" and finally, "Does she lie there kind of quiet, or does she go 'oh-oh-oh'?" Spitting out his breakfast, Burns yells, "Keep your filthy mouth to yourself," and then he jumps Hawkeye. Trapper of course adds fuel to the fire, shouting, "Watch out for your goodies, Hawkeye, that man is a sex maniac, I don't think Hot Lips satisfied him!" So the pitiable Burns is removed from camp. Altman quickly stops the scene from becoming remorseful, or from allowing the viewer to think that Hawkeye and Trapper were too cruel in their treatment of the man, by having Duke immediately confront Henry Blake, saying, "Colonel, fair is fair. If I nail Hot Lips and punch Hawkeye, can I go home?" Thus the surgeons end up doing Burns a favor by getting him out of Korea.

Once Burns is gone, the film becomes even more loosely episodic than it has been, consisting of six major sequences: the Last Supper; the Hot Lips shower scene; the drafting of Ho-Jon (Kim Atwood); the trip to Tokyo; the football game; and the departure of Hawkeye and Duke. The episodes provide succinct examples of the treatment of religion, war, sex, and hypocrisy in the film as the surgeons continue to outrage tradition.

The Last Supper sequence is perhaps the most outrageous bit in *M*A*S*H*, but the object of the satire here is not religion, as one would suspect, but it is instead war films per se. The subtext in this episode, in which the Painless Pole attempts suicide, is that war films never mock the religious beliefs or rituals of soldiers. Faith and religion are always vindicated, as in *The Fighting 69th* or in the films mentioned in the loudspeaker announcements of *M*A*S*H*—*When Willie Comes Marching Home* or *The Glory Brigade*. This is also why the introduction to Frank Burns is bizarre and unsettling, when he mentions to Hawkeye and Duke, "The list grows longer every day—now I have your souls to pray for." Altman's ethics are more situational than antireligious. Dago Red, for example, is a figure of parody not just because he is a priest, but because he is simply a nice man trying to deal with the insanity and immorality around him by ignoring it. So he pretends he does not find the underwear of Lieutenant Dish on the ground, and he thinks that the broadcast lovemaking of Burns and Houlihan is in fact an episode of the radio show "The Battling Bickersons." He is therefore also content with absolving Painless from the "intention" of committing suicide and with giving a solemn blessing to the jeep that Hawkeye will drive when he leaves the unit.

The surgeons have a field day with their ludicrously serious patient Painless, who feels compelled to kill himself because of his occasional impotence—he fears he is becoming a homosexual. So they invent their black capsule ("it worked for Hitler and Eva Braun"), and conduct an irreverent eulogy before setting him in his coffin. The language of this send-off for Painless is filled with tongue-in-cheek military clichés. For example, Duke intones, "You know, I've got an idea that maybe it's not such a final farewell after all. I think maybe ol' Walt's goin' on to the unknown and do a little recon work for us all." Hawkeye then adds, "Nobody ordered Walt to go on this mission—he volunteered, certain death, that's what we award our finest medals for, that's what being a soldier is all about." But after hearing the theme song, "Suicide Is Painless," the viewer is left with essentially a downbeat situation—everyone has filed past the corpse and the coffin is carried out of the tent. Altman again rescues the scene from its own sobriety with the conversation between Hawkeye and Lieutenant Dish, when he convinces her to be of some service to Walt by performing a "simple act of charity."

This process of following a big joke with a letdown and ending with a less somber but still thought-provoking conclusion is repeated in the Hot Lips shower scene. The timing and execution of the stunt are funnier than the content, which is the physical exposition of Hot Lips to the camp. Although her reaction is overblown, Hot Lips makes some serious and truthful charges in Colonel Blake's tent. The staging of the scene, with Blake in bed drinking champagne with a nurse, lessens the tension, which is further deflated when Blake calls her bluff about resigning her commission.

On the occasion when Ho-Jon is inducted into the Korean Army, the technique of the director is self-reflexive. Altman films Hawkeye, who is shocked by the loss of his friend, from the point of view of a female journalist, while she films him standing in his jeep, with her 16mm Bell and Howell camera. She asks if he wants to say hello to his mother, and the scene ends as abruptly as it began, with Hawkeye saying, "Hi, Dad" into her camera as she is driven past him. It is the most human and personal moment for Hawkeye in the entire film, and it clearly establishes him as the central, thoughtful, and lonely protagonist of *M*A*S*H*.

The next event for Hawkeye and Trapper is their trip to Tokyo, and it is perhaps the funniest and best-sustained comic sequence in the film. Trapper receives an invitation to operate in Tokyo while he and Hawkeye are practicing their golf game, using the helicopter landing pad as the driving range. The scene begins with a stunning overhead shot; once he hears the news, Trapper takes Hawkeye by the arm and says, "How often can you go to Tokyo with your golf clubs? C'mon, Shirley." In the very next shot they are being driven to the Tokyo hospital by an exasperated sergeant. They push their way into the operating room, with Trapper issuing nonstop orders, demanding "at least one nurse who knows how to work in close without her tits getting in the way." During the operation Hawkeye is surprised to find that the anesthetist is Me Lay Marston (Michael Murphy), an old friend of his, but Hawkeye does not recognize him (once again) until Johnson banters, "So why don't you save your rapierlike wit for the clam diggers back home, Hawkeye?" After the operation, between geisha houses and "screwing Kabuki dancers," the "pros from Dover" illegally operate to save the life of a Japanese infant. The foppish base colonel declares, "This time I will not be intimidated," thus informing the viewer that this is exactly what is going to occur. Johnson anesthetizes the colonel, and with his help Hawkeye and Trapper quickly blackmail him. Having saved two lives they arrive back at the 4077th wearing new golf clothes and operate immediately while still in their spiked shoes.

Altman begins the "symbolic" football game sarcastically enough. General Hammond (G. Wood) tells Henry that an intersquad football game is "the best way of keeping the American way of life going in Asia." The game itself is rather clichéd, featuring the cameo appearances of Fran Tarkenton, Ben Davidson, and Jack Concannon, along with the *M*A*S*H* "ringer," Captain Oliver Wendell "Spearchucker" Jones (Fred Williamson). Hot Lips is now a team player, having had an affair with Duke, and she leads cheers with an amusing naïveté: at the sound of the halftime gun she screams, "My God, they shot him!" The sequence, however, is overly long, and the humor is mostly surface and slapstick, heavy-handed at that.

For a film of such complexities, loose ideas, and fragile humor, Altman handles the ending extremely effectively. The flash-forward of Duke arriving in the United States, the mixed feelings of Hawkeye—elation and sadness, about leaving his friends—are underplayed, not too sentimental. When Hawkeye tells Duke they can leave, for instance, another surgeon who is assisting Duke in the operating room asks plaintively, "Do you mind if we get out of this guy's brains first?" As they depart, the colonel asks Radar if they stole the jeep. Radar's response, "No sir, that's the one they came in," recalls the skewed logic of the *M*A*S*H* world, to which Hawkeye was a major contributor—a logic that is emphasized again in the final public-address announcement, "Tonight's movie has been *M*A*S*H*. Follow the zany antics of our combat surgeons . . . snatching love and laughter between amputations and penicillin."

The Authorship Controversy

One aspect of *M*A*S*H* that received much attention upon its release in 1970 was the use of overlapping dialogue, a habit that Altman had refined at the cost of many jobs in television and film. The multiple conversations in *M*A*S*H* are witty and acerbic: their effectiveness is also a result of the director's pacing and his ear for colloquialisms. Much of the repartee, and many of the humorous insults, propositions, and sarcastic interjections, however, were Lardner's words. Altman's timing and writing, and Lardner's comic dialogue, constituted the unusually rich aural qualities of *M*A*S*H*, and caused serious disagreements between the director and the screenwriter about the importance of the screenplay. The controversy, of course, centered on who was more responsible for the success of *M*A*S*H*. Altman stated, with a sense of irony, that "my main contribution to *M*A*S*H* was the concept, the philosophy, the style, the casting, and then making all those things work. Plus the jokes, of course," while Lardner believed that the screenplay he wrote "was almost completely the same" as the film.[3]

Both opinions reflect somewhat extreme stances, each with serious implications. Altman placed himself in the unfortunate theoretical position of understating the importance of *M*A*S*H* as a collaborative experience. One the other hand, Lardner overestimated the importance of his script, and he ignored the fact that Altman did not adhere rigidly to that script or to the original novel.

A comparison of the film's dialogue with the original Lardner work indicates some truth in both points of view. Lardner's hand is most evident in two sequences that Altman retained nearly intact: the eavesdropping on Burns and Houlihan, and the Houlihan shower scene. Neither incident appears in the Hooker novel. In addition, Ring Lardner stated that the seemingly spontaneous humor and improvisations were Robert Altman's doing, but this rather significant admission does not only apply to the overlapping dialogue. The first and last few scenes of the film, for example, are found neither in the Lardner script nor in the Hooker novel. Similarly, most of the operating-room byplay, many sarcastic comments of Hawkeye and Trapper, the verbal confusion between Henry and Radar, and the treatment of the colonel in Tokyo were written and orchestrated by the director, and by the actors under his supervision, not by Ring Lardner, Jr.

An accurate stance on the authorship issue in *M*A*S*H* requires some mediation between the two expressed opinions. A joke that is a clear example of the type of writer-director collaboration that occurred commonly throughout the film is the brief exchange between Houlihan and Mulcahy, where the chaplain answers, "He was drafted." Altman kept the lines as they were scripted by Lardner. It is, of course, the speed of the response and quick cutting between the two characters that accentuated the cynical humor. Lardner's contribution cannot be ignored, but it is a fact that Altman was the more important influence in organizing and controlling the comedy and pathos of the *M*A*S*H* project. Just as Welles benefited from the participation of his writer and crew to create *Citizen Kane*, Robert Altman shaped his source work into a coherent, complex expression of a particular artistic vision with the input of his own writer, producers, performers, and crew.

Reception

At the time of its release the film was daring, shocking, and inventive, so much so that it originally received an "X" rating, which was protested and changed. It played very well to both extremes of audiences: younger, hip audiences applauded its relevance to Vietnam, while more traditional factions were amused by its negative treatment of military red tape and bureaucracy. The operating-room scenes, filled with spurting arteries, open chests, and detached limbs, disturbed most viewers; even more shocking was the surgeons' casual attitude toward their work. Their critical approach to the Korean conflict, to religion, and to hypocrisy defined an antiwar message even though no battles are in evidence in the film. Its ironic context, established by the captioned Eisenhower quotation, "I will go to Korea," appealed to most viewers, while suggesting also that military presence produces only one tangible consequence—the production of wounded and dead soldiers.

M*A*S*H certainly received more immediate critical acclaim than most of Altman's later films. Jan Dawson described in *Sight and Sound* how *M*A*S*H* "demands to be taken, on its own empirical terms, as probably one of the most irreducibly funny films ever made,"[4] while William Johnson in *Film Quarterly* concluded that the film "is not really about army life or rebellion . . . it is about the human condition, and that's why it is such an exciting comedy."[5] Pauline Kael's evaluation typified the reviews of *M*A*S*H* when she called it "a marvelously unstable comedy, a tough, funny, and sophisticated burlesque of military attitudes."[6]

Richard Corliss, on the other hand, thought that the film was unsuccessful and amoral, objecting that *M*A*S*H* was just another exploitation film that leads the audience "to sympathize with the torturers (however likable) and against the victims (however ludicrous)."[7] Basing his argument on the treatment of Burns by Hawkeye and Trapper, Corliss judges the film to be an intentionally cruel and sadistic compilation of cheap shots. Unfortunately Corliss ignores the defusing remark of Duke that shows Burns to be lucky to get out of Korea. Burns is put in a straitjacket because he tries to kill Hawkeye, and laughter results from the total collapse of the moral and religious pretentions of Major Burns, not because he is a victim of torture.

Finally it has been suggested that in comparison to his later films, *M*A*S*H* lacks subtlety. This is an interesting permutation of the usual criticism of Altman—that the director has been trying to recapture the success of *M*A*S*H* in his later films—but the charge is still not sensible. Altman never had the same goals for later films as he had for *M*A*S*H*. His technique is more disjointed in *M*A*S*H*, but it is certainly not crude. Altman would never make another film quite like *M*A*S*H*. It demands to be judged on its own merits.

M*A*S*H grossed over $30 million for Fox within a year of its release. It won the 1970 New York Film Critics Best Picture Award. It received Academy Award nominations for Best Supporting Actress (Sally Kellerman), Best Screenplay, Best Director, and Best Film, and won the Best

Screenplay award (to Ring Lardner, Jr., alone). But the most lucrative aspect of *M*A*S*H* was the 1971 television spinoff by Gene Reynolds and Larry Gelbart. *M*A*S*H*'s episodic nature ideally suited it for this transformation. The language was laundered, the actors were changed (except for Gary Burghoff), and the show was quickly put into simultaneous syndication, all of which generated massive revenues for everyone concerned except Robert Altman. The director received his $75,000 fee for making the picture and nothing from the series, apart from the royalties received by his son, who wrote the lyrics to the theme song. In fact, Altman considered the twelve-year prolongation of any joke about war to be an immoral proposition, regardless of the orientation, perspective, or tone of the show.

M*A*S*H was another turning point in the career of Robert Altman. Now recognized as a major talent, he received many offers to do big-budget studio productions. Swamped with lucrative deals and unsolicited screen plays, he chose to abandon the studios and to set out on his own. His choice here was similar to his decision to quit television in spite of his $125,000 yearly income. If he had stayed in Hollywood, the artistic freedom he had struggled for fifteen years to achieve would be eroded or usurped. Financial rewards would have been greater, but studio domination would have proved an insurmountable obstacle. He opted therefore to experiment with his own small projects. By the autumn of 1969 he had already established postproduction facilities and offices in Westwood in Los Angeles. With his technical assistants, including Robert Eggenweiler, Scottie Bushnell, and Tommy Thompson, he solidified Lion's Gate Films, Ltd., and their first production was *Brewster McCloud*.

3

Brewster McCloud

ROBERT ALTMAN ONCE NAMED *Brewster McCloud* as a personal favorite of his films.[1] Considering his fascination with the subject of freedom in America, the choice is understandable. Like *Quintet*, the film celebrates an indomitable life force. Like *McCabe and Mrs. Miller*, it praises the fragile dreams, passions, and contradictions to which its hero clings.

Story Line

At first glance the story appears chaotic, with its slapstick humor, ludicrous conversations, and broad "comic book" parodies. Altman kept most scenes in the film short and funny. On ocasions in-jokes are too obscure, discussions too verbose, the cynical tone too distracting. But for the most part, the fast pace and outrageousness of *Brewster* work well for Altman. His characters seem to emerge from *Mad* magazine, but their misbegotten strategies and oddly compulsive antics are genuinely disturbing and suggest a fundamental failing of our culture to preserve the dignity and freedom of the individual.

The style of *Brewster McCloud* illustrates how Altman, freed from the schedules and pressures of his television days and from his confinement to studio shooting, began experimenting with visual narrative, testing and improvising in ways that significantly influenced the development of plot in later films. The themes of hypocrisy and self-delusion recur in *Nashville* and *Three Women*, for example, without the "sugar coating" he provides for *Brewster*. Yet for all its problems of characterization, narrative organizations, and simple-minded humor, *Brewster* nonetheless succeeds as a quick-paced, irreverent allegory of a society that treats its nonconformists as enemies. As such, *Brewster* represents a major step forward in the film career of Robert Altman.

Brewster McCloud relates the activities of a young man named Brewster (Bud Cort) who lives in a fallout shelter in the Houston Astrodome. His life centers on the construction of a large pair of mechanical wings, with which he hopes to fly. He is aided by Louise (Sally Kellerman), who

Bud Cort as Brewster McCloud spreads his wings in the Astrodome. Courtesy of Warner Bros., Burbank, CA.

provides him with encouragement and protection. Her dedication seems boundless: she assists him in murdering anyone who threatens him or the security of his project. The story of Brewster's relationships and his progress with the wings is punctuated with human-avian comparisons by the Lecturer (René Auberjonois), whose ironic commentary pokes fun at the characters. His remarks are also used to justify the logic and importance of Brewster's life and schemes.

An influential businessman named Haskel Weeks (William Windom) hires Frank Shaft (Michael Murphy), a famous San Francisco detective, to curtail that series of murders. Suzanne (Shelley Duvall), an Astrodome tour guide, helps Brewster elude Shaft, but she eventually betrays Brewster by reporting his location to Weeks. Brewster then kills Weeks. Wearing his completed wings, Brewster leaps from an Astrodome balcony and flies for a brief time before falling to his death.

Robert Altman had dealt with such subject matter before. The film bears a remarkable thematic resemblance to a project entitled "The Dream Riders," directed for television by Altman and aired on "Bonanza." Based on a script of the same name by Jack McCann and James Von Wagoner, it told the story of Major Cayley bringing an unusual project to Virginia City. Cayley explains to Adam the "miracle of his concept"—that a man could escape the boundaries of the earth through flight. The Major hoped to achieve this goal in a helium balloon. Adam marvels at the boldness of his idea, but tells him, "It's a nice thought. But I'm afraid the sky will always belong to the birds and angels." Undaunted by Adam's parochialism, Cayley attempts flight after robbing a bank, and is killed. Adam conjectures that Cayley was a victim of his own madness, but Ben refutes this theory. Like the Lecturer of *Brewster* Ben declares that although the dreamer is dead, "the dream made it." Ben reflects that "he's riding his dream across the sky, just as he said he would." In *Brewster*, the Lecturer makes similar closing comments about the resurrection of the dreamer.

Nearly ten years after the "Bonanza" episode, Altman seized upon that same concept in a script by Doran William Cannon,[2] entitled *Brewster McLeod's Flying Machine*. Altman was still attracted to the idea that a man might be obsessed with a primal urge for freedom through flight, so he used the Cannon treatment as a point of departure. Since *Brewster McCloud* was an experiment for Altman, it was done "in a very fragmented style," with his lack of allegiance to the script indicated in his appraisal that "the script we went by was something nobody really saw." That observation was also borne out in C. Kirk McClelland's diary of the production of *Brewster*.[3] Ultimately, the only elements of the Cannon treatment retained in the film were the name of the main character and an idea (consistent also with the "Bonanza" project) of "the kid flying."[4] The most drastic change from Cannon's story, besides the shift from New York City to Houston, involved the personality of Brewster. By casting Bud Cort, with his "adolescent naive countenance,"[5] as Brewster, and by having the murders occur offscreen, the director eliminated the prurient and sadomasochistic aspects of the Cannon protagonist.

The story also changed as cast members began to contribute their personal background to their roles in the film. Stacy Keach, for example, had previously appeared in *Orville and Wilbur*, a play for National Educational Television. In *Brewster* he portarys Abraham Wright, a third Wright brother. With informed input from his actors, Altman wrote new scenes and dialogue the night before they were to be filmed—a practice that the director maintained in his subsequent films.

There are two discernible narrative patterns to the initially puzzling series of events and characters of *Brewster McCloud*. The primary narrative structure is mythic. Altman's hero struggles to free himself from the madness and absurdity he perceives around him. With the monomania of Ahab, the careful logic of Dedalus, and the impetuousness of Icarus, this gullible young man tries to escape a corrupt and destructive society. He fights so that someday he may achieve "real flying," and it is ironic that this flight is only attempted within the confined space of the Astrodome. He overcomes obstacles (i.e., John Shaft), experiences rites of passage (with Suzanne), and seeks refuge in a cavelike retreat until he is ready to bring his gift (of "real flying") to humanity. He undertakes a journey of the spirit (the film's dream sequence). He faces prophecies of doom and, after being betrayed by friends, he hopes for rebirth through his death. According to the Lecturer, Brewster invents "subtleties and refinements of man's clumsy progress" through life.

The events in *Brewster* are also arranged in such a way as to indicate why that "progress" in general is in fact so "clumsy." Each character in turn falls prey to a specific obsession—wealth, power, and prestige. The narrative then follows how they pursue their objectives and destroy themselves. Their jaded schemes are at times compared with Brewster's more noble ambition. Haskel Weeks's plan to accrue financial and political power, for example, leads to his undoing. The goals of Brewster—his desires for freedom and for a stable romantic relationship— result just as certainly in his annihilation. Weeks's death is of little significance. Brewster's death, on the other hand, accentuates the worthiness of his pursuit of freedom and valiance of his struggle. Each scene is recorded in deadpan fashion. The most outrageous activities and events in *Brewster McCloud* are defined as essentially perverted but not really unusual because of the free-for-all atmosphere propagated by the "hardnosed realists"[6] of the film.

Each succeeding death closely follows that narrative pattern, captured in the starkest terms possible. Daphne Heap (Margaret Hamilton), finally seen in red slippers recollecting the actress's role in *The Wizard of Oz*, dies because of her ludicrous "deep affection" for "prize pigeons." Her elegantly costumed corpse has been littered by pigeons flying in her garden. The viewer begins to suspect in this scene that Heap may have in fact deserved this harsh, cynical treatment, because of her allusive relationship to "the wicked witch"; her murder (by Brewster and Louise) thus becomes less repulsive to the viewer.

The dialogue between the miserly landlord Abraham Wright, who employs Brewster as a chauffeur, and Wright's tenant Bertie (Verdie Henshaw) at the "Feathered Nest Sanitarium" quickly reveals his sole and lifelong concern for money. Wright wrestles with Bertie, yelling, "Hah—look at that—two big Georges right there," and rips a few dollars from under her blouse. He shouts, "Look at that, there's money right there in your hand," and he pulls a wig from the elderly woman's head. Wright's obsession with money and his unconscionable methods of pursuing wealth lead directly to his death. Again, Altman chooses to depict the death in an appropriately degrading manner. While exiting from a nursery home in his wheelchair, he drops a bundle of money on the ground. When Brewster begins to gather the bills for him, Wright aims a pistol at Brewster and warns, "Don't you ever lay a hand on my money." A birdcall warns of another death and the scene cuts to Wright careening down a hill in his wheelchair, narrowly missing cars. With a country-western song on the soundtrack, the viewer hears, "All that funny money / It won't get you milk and honey." The lyrics summarize the cause of Wright's demise. The entire scene, in fact, encourages delight in Wright's murder. The technique is not simply graveyard humor. The detached treatment of the scene signals another attempt to "turn tables" on the viewer, pushing the viewer first to laugh at the person's humiliation, as in $M*A*S*H II$, then to be appalled at the success of the joke.

When inveterate race-car driver Billy Joe Goodwill falsely accuses Brewster of stealing the automobile that Suzanne has appropriated, Brewster's nonchalant "I think you made an error" is the last straw for Goodwill, who yells, "Now I'm fixin' to scrum your head." The birdcall signals that Goodwill's affection for his racing car will result in his death. Again Altman treats the scene in such a matter-of-fact tone that the viewer believes Brewster is not really implicated in a murder—that the "innocent" Brewster had meted out a just punishment in a reasonable manner.

The obsessions thus far in the film concerned little more than prized possessions and greed. The deaths of Shaft and Weeks, however, have their basis in more complex motivations: the characters' blind pursuit of an ideology and their overwhelming desire for fame and political power. The victim of ideological tunnel vision is Frank Shaft. Shaft, "San Francisco's supercop," believes that life's highest priority should be the progressive circumscription of lawbreakers. His comments to his partner Lt. Alvin Johnson (John Schuck), reveal that basic philosophy. Shaft reminds him, "There's a killer on the loose. Are we gonna go get him, or are we gonna go downtown and play politics?" A "whale of a cop" or not, Shaft's rigid adherence to that code proves a source of embarrassment to those "downtown" officials. Ignoring Johnson's suggestion to meet with Crandall and Weeks, Shaft refuses to be deterred from his assignment. His conversations with Weeks illustrate his myopia. When Weeks invites him to dinner, he answers, "I'll be busy." To Weeks's insinuation, "My friends are not without influence," Shaft quips, "Good, then they won't miss me." He later tells Weeks, "I really don't have time for this small talk," and warns Crandall, "You go ahead and do your 'old-fashioned police work,' Captain, and leave me alone to work my way."

Frustrated at every turn by those whom he obviously regards as incompetents, Shaft solicits Johnson's help. He explains with mathematical precision his plan for spotting the Goodwill car, exuding confidence in his masterstroke. The chase, however, ends contrary to his expectations: the supercop's car rams through a garage, swerves across a park lawn, and crashes into a pond. When a photographer approaches the submerged car and offers assistance to Shaft, who is now missing one of his blue contact lenses, he responds, "That won't be necessary." A single gunshot then occurs in the car. Altman casually implies that Shaft's solution, again, is perfectly reasonable—that there is nothing wrong with the price Shaft pays for failure in his mission. The revelation of suicide is so offhand that it nearly passes unnoticed. This portrayal of bizarre events as routine is the satiric tool Altman uses in *M*A*S*H*, *The Long Goodbye*, *Nashville*, *A Wedding*, *Health*, and to some degree, *Popeye*.

Brewster's obsessive pursuit of freedom, however, is the crux of the film. It is his tragic story of hopes and inventions that captures the viewer's sympathies. He is a gullible, compulsive dreamer. He loves Suzanne, who betrays him; he trusts Louise, who deceives him. So fervently does he abide by his dream of "real flying" that he forsakes his life in an attempt to separate himself from the encroachments of a hostile world.

The Lecturer stresses the conflict central to Brewster's struggle: that "the desire to fly is ever present in the mind of man, but the reality has been long in coming." Brewster desires to close that gap by "building my wings." Once he leaves the employment of Abraham Wright, that task consumes all his time and effort. He constructs wings based on detailed photographs of birds at rest and in flight. Living in his workshop, Brewster prepares for flight through constant physical exercise. Louise expresses concern over Brewster's routine, telling him, "Come on, we have to stay on schedule . . . don't let anything take your full concentration from your work." She reinforces his notion that one can indeed transcend reality through flight.

Brewster in fact needs little encouragement: the tragic flaw in his character involves his disregard for any information that might distract him from his goal. When Suzanne tells him how he can capitalize on his project, stressing the financial rewards of such a venture, he comments, "Suzanne, you're talking crazy." Only when she agrees to fly with him is Brewster's confidence in her restored.

Brewster now views Louise as a burden and tells her to leave. By crosscutting between this rejection and the bedroom scene with Suzanne, the director suggests a connection between his sexual awakening and his breaking away from his surrogate mother, Louise. Brewster erroneously accepts this sensation as true love. His naïveté was previously evident in his bathtub scene wtih Louise, when she explains that "all people want to fly until it comes to sex." His affair with Suzanne then teaches him that sexual involvement (love, for Brewster) is both compatible and complementary to his desire to fly. When she betrays him, the soundtrack, without much subtlety, repeats the lyric, "I pretended not to see," echoing the misjudgments and false assumptions that defeat Brewster.

Thematic development in *Brewster McCloud* hinges on a comparison between the deluded Brewster and the realists of the film. The dreamer finds sadness and death, but the realist fares no better. Brewster chooses to fly above the "aweful abyss," while others wallow in the mundane. The methodological approach of Frank Shaft toward the solution of the crime emphasizes the tenuousness of a realist philosophy in *Brewster*. His attempt to gather a description of the murderer from the butler Milhaus (Ellis Gilbert) severely tests the adequacy of scientific pragmatism. The comic scene demonstrates the absurdity of rational thought in a world skewed from that perspective. Shaft first asks, "How tall was he?" Milhaus replies, "Oh short, very short, like you." Shaft objects, "I'm 6'1", Milhaus," and Milhaus, genuinely surprised, asks, "You are? I'm 5'9" and you look shorter than me." Shaft slowly explains, as if to a child, "You're standing on the steps." Shaft reasons, "Steps are about 8"," and their conversation continues: soon Shaft is forced to conclude that the murderer was three feet, five inches tall, to which Milhaus quickly agrees, "That's right, he was short, like you." Shaft's attempt to impose logic on what is patently absurd is ludicrous. The fruitlessness of his method of inquiry in this scene rivals the breakdown of Cartesian analysis parodied by Samuel Beckett in *Molloy* and *Watt*.

Shaft's investigation later depends on the availability of an avian scatologist in the Houston area. His superior, Captain Crandall (G. Wood), makes no headway with "old-fashioned police work." Shaft's liaison, Lt. Johnson, is too confounded by Shaft's prestige to advance any significant theories about the murderer. In each case, the person with more "practical" notions than Brewster's is trapped by his own fetishes. With each en-

Befuddled detectives on the trail of the mysterious killer in Brewster McCloud.
Courtesy of Warner Bros., Burbank, CA.

counter, Brewster's approach to life grows more enviable.

The "scientific" pose of the Lecturer lends additional credence to Brewster's perspective. Like Opal in *Nashville*, the Lecturer serves as an intermittent narrator and as a figure of self-parody for Altman. The Lecturer, however, is never specifically involved in the events of the film. The close interrelationship of characters evident in the conclusion of *Nashville* is missing from *Brewster*. The Lecturer remains "tacked on" to the large narrative; the attempt at self-parody (i.e., the director mimicking the absurdity of his own story) falls short of its mark. The Lecturer also distances the viewer from the events in the film—a function similar to the voice-over in *M*A*S*H*, the opening television sequence in *California Split*, the comic-book introduction to *Nashville*, and the voice-over narration of the Old Soldier at the beginning of *Buffalo Bill*. Indeed the main character in *Brewster* exists in a world apart from the audience; Altman seems intent upon developing an awareness of the fiction of this film.

Experimental Techniques

The pace and atmosphere of the film are also shaped by the director's experimentation with editing and sound. Few shots in the first twenty-five scenes of the film are held for longer than fifteen seconds; most of those scenes are shorter than a minute. A scene typically opens with a voice-over introduction, a brief conversation containing several cutaway and reaction shots followed by a new voice-over, commencing before the scene is completed. The tour-guide scenes in the Astrodome are cross-cut with the first conversation of Shaft and Johnson, establishing the immediacy and spontaneity of the setting in *Brewster*. Quick transitions through cross-cutting reinforce the atmosphere of a world gone mad: telephones ring, sirens blast, and radios blurt meaningless phrases throughout the opening of the film.

The pace slackens when Altman begins characterizing Brewster, but cross-cutting continues as the mainstay of narrative technique in *Brewster*. It well befits the comic exchanges and subjects of pursuit and flight. The dialogue between Shaft and Milhaus is cross-cut with Brewster's encounter with Douglas Breen (Bert Remsen) at the zoo. The telephone conversation between Shaft and Johnson is paralleled with Brewster and Louise's bathtub scene. Suzanne's first meeting with Brewster occurs in the middle of Breen's funeral. Brewster and Suzanne's arrival at the amusement park visually coincides with Shaft's instruction to Johnson on apprehending the murderer. The physical appearance of the Lecturer deteriorates as Brewster's death approaches.

Altman also makes effective use of overlapping dialogue in *Brewster McCloud*. The director hoped that it would provide "indirect buttressing" for the action, establishing a feeling "that there were things outside of the frame that supported the things that were in the frame." Shaft's discussion with a laboratory technician, for example, is interrupted by the remarks of Weeks and Crandall. The technician begins by describing the type of animal excrement found on the corpse of Breen. He attempts to formulate a specific theory from the three simultaneous conversations. The technician begins, "It might not have even come from a bird," but then we hear the statement from Weeks, "I'll assume I did not hear that." Shaft meanwhile addresses the technician with "What else could have," and Weeks asks, to no one in particular, "So will you pop in?" The criminology laboratory analysis scene thus becomes an informal social gathering.

This loss of order, suggested by the overlapping dialogue, is also evident at the investigation of the death of Billy Joe Goodwill. A detective asks, "Can you tell me when the guy died?" but Crandall answers, "To hell with the widow Green!" A second detective, describing Shaft, says, "He's got a very good reputation," while Crandall still wonders about the cause of death. The detective continues, "The Santa Barbara murderer surrendered to him," and Crandall loses his patience. The audible dialogue here presents some reference points; the rambling background vocal track, however, is often more interesting to the viewer. In this conversation the director suggests an identification with the befuddled Crandall. So much is said at once that Crandall seems to be the only person with a normal reaction to the chaos. Once that transitory identification is made, the director can shape the viewer's perceptions through Crandall's cynical point of view. The overlapping dialogue thus prejudices the viewer against this group of "realists."

The mise-en-scène communicates the limited freedom of the protagonist. Brewster is primarily trapped in the "enormous environmental enclosure" of the Astrodome. Altman makes "the weight of the earth's imprisonment" upon Brewster more evident by framing him against fallout shelter walls and ceiling; by trapping him in cars and on stairways; and by perching him on an Astrodome balcony, with the exits blocked by the police. To a large extent, the opening gambit of repeating the film's titles sets the stage for the incongruities and parodies that follow. Wright's interactions are either extremely polite, or barbaric ("Get out of my way, you silly bitch, or I'll mow you down"). Billy Joe Goodwill is seen swinging a motorcycle chain, but he is wearing a "Porky Pig" T-shirt. These characters are hypocrites. Their actions are in many ways more ludicrous than Brewster's.

The extensive parodies in *Brewster* include the satire of police in gangster films. Law-enforcement agents in *Brewster* suffer either from physical and mental incompetence or from overzealousness. Frank Shaft, for example, gives haywire instructions to Johnson for catching Brewster: "All right, Johnson, here it is. Take Memorial to West Loop South. Take West Loop South to South of East. I'll go out 59 to Post Oak Road, and I'll meet you on West Loop South." Of course Shaft never meets Johnson on West Loop South; Johnson's grimaces suggest that although he is trying, he does not understand a word of the proposal. Altman thus reiterates the disintegration of logic in *Brewster McCloud*.

Altman uses clichés to turn the Houston police force into the Keystone Kops of the 1970s. An all-points bulletin begins with "Calling all cars" and ends with "y'all." Before and during the chase scene, the viewer hears "The occupant is considered dangerous," "Don't be heroic," and "Follow that car!" The chase scene itself reinforces that negative impression. Although he is engrossed in a *Captain America* comic book, Johnson notices the suspect car. He reports, "I've spotted them . . . I'm traveling incognito," which is when Suzanne sees the squad car. The chase begins, appropriately enough, at an amusement park.

The scene was obviously modeled after Peter Yates's epic chase sequence in *Bullitt*. Excitement mounts when the drivers buckle their seatbelts, but this incipient tension gives way to comedy when Altman cuts to country-western music. After several telescopic-lens shots and an extended sequence of cars flying over the crest of a hill, Shaft's car crashes and Brewster escapes. Bullitt walked away from his car crash, but Shaft remains in his car, which is sinking into a pond.

The parodies in *Brewster* generally rely on this facile type of slapstick comedy, but at times the satire takes on a higher level of significance. For example, one may read the warning of the Lecturer to "draw no conclusions" in the same vein as Mark Twain's "Notice to the Reader" at the beginning of *Huckleberry Finn*. Like Twain, Altman attempts to warn his audience of the idiosyncrasies and delusions they may share with his characters.

When asked to describe his thoughts on *Brewster McCloud*, Altman stated, "I know the stuff in it is good, but whether the whole picture together is going to work or not is questionable." The film does work in spite of its strange events, the problematic presence of the Lecturer, and a too-lengthy dream sequence. Two shortcomings, however, nearly jeopardize the aesthetic integrity of the film: a lack of emotional capacity in the character of Brewster, and the absence of a time scheme in the film.

Since the film describes Brewster's unusual dream and his strategy for achieving that ambition, the viewer should have some access to his thoughts and emotions. The viewer can surmise his motivation, but his emotions are a mystery. The number of close-ups of Brewster is limited. His statement of trust in Louise and his neutral dismissal of her show little involvement. Altman consistently refuses to light any fire under Brewster. Even in his death scene, Brewster's face reflects only physical strain. His final vocalizations are the death throes of a trapped animal. Emotional identification with this "crazy person" is very difficult.

The cross-cutting, the parallel editing, and the constantly moving camera do remind the viewer that more is happening to Brewster than Altman chooses to frame. To heighten this stylized drama, Altman consciously forces the viewer to ignore the importance of time. Events affecting Brewster occur within a two-day period but there is only one fleeting reference to time within the film. This temporal disregard often obscures the sequence of events in the film.

But even with these misjudgments by the director, the film remains a daring, complex, and enjoyable experiment in a significant thematic and narrative style that would carry Altman through many films. The visual format of many scenes in *Brewster* closely resembles the style of his later films, suggesting that the narrative and cinematographic devices most important to the director were forged in *Brewster McCloud*. Like *California*

Split, *Nashville*, and *Buffalo Bill*, *Brewster* begins with a comic evocation of patriotism and American ideals. The opening scenes of *McCabe and Mrs. Miller* and *Thieves Like Us* are close approximations of *Brewster's* beginning: a long pan, followed by three different establishing shots and a close-up on the main character. *Brewster* initiates Altman's extensive use of voice-over narration, employed occasionally in *M*A*S*H* and retained in *California Split*, *Nashville*, and *Buffalo Bill*.

On two occasions in *Brewster* a humorous effect is achieved through the pairing of country-western music with a montage of cars colliding. This technique is repeated in the two collisions in *Nashville*, when cars crash through parking-lot gates "accompanied by some fast picking music," and when a couch, which has fallen from a car on a freeway, causes "a mass of screeching, sliding and crashing," with the same background music. The traffic collisions are an amusing form of self-destruction for Altman, and his characters need a retreat from that type of insanity. Consequently Brewster lives in a fallout shelter. This need for isolation is felt by Cathryn, who escapes the perceived pressures and deceit surrounding her by creating a fantasy world in *Images*. T-Dub in *Thieves* desires to flee to New Jersey and hide out on "that little farm and let the mistletoe hang on my coattail for rest of the world." The desire for security and for a retreat finds full expression in Barbara Jean's hope to return to "my Idaho home" in *Nashville*.

Brewster's inability to view the facts of his existence in a practical manner results in his death. Like John McCabe and Buffalo Bill, Brewster seeks to align an immutable reality with his dream. Brewster, for example, is aware of certain physical laws governing flight. He adheres steadfastly to them when building his wings, but he ignores the logical conclusion that those wings cannot sustain prolonged flight. He foresees only the transcendence of those laws by sheer willpower and imagination. When Brewster leaves his place of retreat and enters an implacable and hostile environment, with only his dream to protect himself, he is doomed. In *Brewster*, and in each successive Altman film except *Popeye*, no effort of will can stop those forces.

If the viewer, however, heeds the Lecturer's warning and draws conclusions cautiously, the film may still be regarded as a good parable of human spirit enduring the cruelty of a comically hostile world. *Brewster* was an experiment in theme and visual format. The film demonstrates well what Pauline Kael calls the director's "essentially impractical approach to filmmaking."[7] With *Brewster McCloud*, Altman clearly announces that from now on he is going to make films his own way, and the viewer can either enjoy these eccentricities or not, as he chooses.

4

McCabe and Mrs. Miller

McCABE AND MRS. MILLER defies easy categorization in the context of Altman films. It cannot be regarded as one of his strictly "personal" experiments such as *Images*. It does not subject the viewer to the unrelenting emotional battering one finds in *Images*, *Three Women*, and *Jimmy Dean*. The narrative of *McCabe* hardly resembles the rambling "arena approach" evident in *M*A*S*H*, nor does it feature a menagerie of characters, as does *Nashville*, *A Wedding*, *Health*, and *Popeye*.

McCabe and Mrs. Miller represents an elegiac blending of Altman's two extremes of storytelling. The probing of basic psychological and emotional constructs of the main characters leads to a larger critical perspective on their times and setting. John McCabe's successes, capitulations, pretensions, and death fundamentally affect the evolution of a simple frontier community. His struggles and defeat suggest a process of moral degeneration inherent in what Altman would regard as the corporate settling of the West. The director freely adapts a series of traditional western events, motifs, and ideals to capture this atypical vision of Manifest Destiny. For Altman the westerner is a gambler, a braggart, a romantic, and a fool. He hopes to maintain a sense of dignity and the legends about his past, even though honor and reputation are illusions.

Story Line

The arrival of John McCabe (Warren Beatty) at the Pacific Northwest mining settlement of Presbyterian Church in 1902 has a disquieting effect on the population of the town. The Chinese workers and the other miners, including Riley Quinn (Jack Riley), Smalley (John Schuck), and Bart Coyle (Bert Remsen), view him with mixed curiosity and suspicion. The saloon owner Sheehan (René Auberjonois) remarks that the stranger has a "big rep" because he killed the gunslinger Bill Rountree.

With his status as a colorful, cunning, and perhaps dangerous "businessman" established in Presbyterian Church, McCabe travels to the nearby town of Bearpaw, where he purchases three prostitutes, with

McCabe (Warren Beatty) arrives in Presbyterian Church.
Courtesy of Warner Bros., Burbank, CA.

35

whom he establishes a makeshift enterprise in three tents next to Shee-han's saloon. He refuses Sheehan's offer "to form a partnership" simply because "partners is what I came up here to get away from."

Business proceeds as usual for McCabe until the day Mrs. Miller (Julie Christie) arrives in town. Constance Miller has journeyed from Bearpaw with another business proposition in mind. Although she fears that Mc-Cabe may be "a man too dumb to see a good proposition when it's put to him," she offers to run "a sporting house with clean girls and clean linen and proper hygiene" for him, if he supplies the capital investment. Wor-ried about being conned, McCabe reluctantly agrees to her plan.

In spite of their frequent business arguments, McCabe's affection for Mrs. Miller grows. Her acceptance of him remains conditional, perhaps influenced by the degree of her opium intoxication.

McCabe rejects an offer by Eugene Sears (Michael Murphy) and Ernie Hollander (Anthony Holland) of the M. H. Harrison-Shaugnessy Mining Company to purchase his business. Later realizing the seriousness of his error in negotiation, he leaves for Bearpaw to reopen discussion with the men, who have since departed for Seattle. Now worried about the possi-bly violent consequences of their sudden departure, he consults Clem Samuels (William Devane), a Bearpaw lawyer. Hoping to profit from the publicity generated by the case, Samuels convinces McCabe that the best solution to his problem is to "enter everything into the district court rec-ords" and to "file a writ of coercion."

McCabe returns to Presbyterian Church, believing that "somebody's got to protect the small businessman from these big companies." Mean-while, the Harrison-Shaugnessy Mining Company has sent Dog Butler (Hugh Millais) and two henchmen to the town in order to eliminate McCabe. Despite Mrs. Miller's warnings and premonitions, McCabe re-mains in Presbyterian Church to face the assassins. The townspeople, dis-tracted by a fire in the church and by the death of minister Elliott (Corey Fischer), are unaware of the battle that goes on between McCabe and the gunfighters.

McCabe kills each of the gunmen in turn, but is fatally wounded by Butler, the last assassin to die. McCabe stumbles to the snow and falls to the ground. The film then turns from McCabe, whose corpse has merged with the frozen landscape of Presbyterian Church, to Mrs Miller, and ends in a close-up of her lying in an opium den, with her face reflected in a prism.

Although the first treatment of *McCabe and Mrs. Miller* was not writ-ten until late in 1969, Altman had been quite familiar with its plot and themes for many years. He directed a television episode of "Bonanza" en-titled "Bank Run," which was aired on 17 November 1960. Based on an N. B. Stone script, "Bank Run" related the story of the Harrison Corporation's claim on a silver mine, owned by Tim O'Brien and located near the Ponderosa border.

In the episode teaser, Mr. Fish, president of the Harrison Bank, Mine, Mill Investment, and Steamship Company, instructs an aide, Mr. Holmes, to acquire the land from O'Brien. Fish tells Holmes that "negotiation is the backbone of our civilization—force him to negotiate." Then, since the company also plans to annex the Ponderosa, the Cartwright family joins forces with the reclusive O'Brien. Little Joe and Hoss devise and successfully carry out a humorous scheme to defend O'Brien and the Ponderosa by simulating a run on the Virginia City Bank. Once the Harrison plan is foiled, Ben Cartwright tells Fish that he will "make a special trip to Washington, and use all the influence I can to have you investigated and jailed." Through personal initiative and legal recourse the small businessman is thus protected from the threats of a powerful and greedy corporation—a theme common to westerns since the 1930s.

The parallels between "Bank Run" and *McCabe and Mrs. Miller*, however, are too striking to be considered merely coincidental. The Harrison Corporation attempted to eliminate an individual (O'Brien) and affect an entire community (the Ponderosa). The Harrison-Shaugnessy Company in *McCabe and Mrs. Miller* encroaches upon the interests of the entrepreneur (John McCabe) and attempts to influence the economic structure of a community (Presbyterian Church) and its zinc mine. Ben seeks to stop the corporation's infringment on his territory by lobbying Congress. McCabe hopes to salvage his business and his life with the assistance of lawyer Clem Samuels.

The idea of an individual fighting against corporate takeover of the western frontier thus had fascinated Altman more than ten years before *McCabe* was produced. This concept began to coalesce for Altman while he was completing the shooting of *Brewster McCloud*. Throughout the making of *Brewster*, Altman was reviewing, selecting, and writing screenplays for future projects. He obtained from George Litto, the agent through whom Ring Lardner had sold his *M*A*S*H* screenplay to Twentieth Century–Fox, another script, written by Brian McKay and based on an Edmund Naughton novel entitled *McCabe*. McKay offered a straightforward adaptation and called it *The Presbyterian Church Wager*.

The first draft, submitted on 7 December 1969, contained only sixty-four scenes. It told the story of John Quincy "Pudgy" McCabe, who established a whorehouse in the small northwestern town of Presbyterian Church. As soon as his business turns a profit, he is shot and killed by the saloon owner Sheehan. Along with a band of hired guns, Sheehan controls the town. McCabe's body is kept on display and photographed as indisputable evidence of Sheehan's authority in Presbyterian Church. The script then called for a dissolve depicting the transition of Presbyterian

Church in the early 1900s into that same town as a "posh residential development of the 1970s."[1] Taken with the ideas he found in the Naughton
novel and McKay script, Altman completed a 120-page screenplay in the
spring of 1970. He eventually changed the title to *McCabe and Mrs. Miller* because the first title was misleading.

Significant departures from McKay's treatment were made in this version of the screenplay. Altman wanted "to take a very standard Western
story with a classic line and do it real or what I felt was real, and destroy
all the myths of heroism." Sheehan thus becomes an ineffectual bartender
and boardinghouse owner. McCabe contends with the Harrison Company's representatives, not with a band of local cutthroats. His life is tied
romantically and professionally with Mrs. Miller: at the moment of his
death, reality also slips from the life of Constance Miller, who abandons
herself to the hallucinations of her opium dream.

Production

This screenplay contained the essence of plot, characterization, and
theme that would be used in the film, but it was still quite far removed
from final script stage. Altman regarded it as a "selling tool" and as "not
much more than a production schedule."[2] With a site in Vancouver, British Columbia, in mind, he and Warner Brothers proceeded to cast the
film. Warner Brothers wanted George C. Scott for McCabe; Altman refused. Jon Voight and Stacy Keach were both considered briefly. By this
time the search had been fully covered in trade papers. Warren Beatty
solicited and pursued Altman and Warner Brothers until he was finally
awarded the role of John McCabe. The remaining major roles, except for
Mrs. Miller and Clem Samuels, were quickly filled by Altman regulars
from *M*A*S*H* and *Brewster McCloud,* including René Auberjonois,
John Schuck, Michael Murphy, Shelley Duvall, Bert Remsen, and Corey
Fischer.

McCabe was shot during a nine-week period in the summer—a practice
Altman would follow in *The Long Goodbye, Nashville, A Wedding,* and
other films. Together with art director Leon Erickson, Altman had directed the crew in building a crude but realistic mining town. The cast then
had moved into the town, which began to develop its own personality.
Then Altman and assistant director Tommy Thompson scouted the area
for camera set-ups that would capture the feeling of the new town.

Shooting began in the West Vancouver area on 22 May 1970, and was
completed on 18 July. The film was shot in sequence, a procedure that
provided the director and the performers with a strong sense of story
continuity.

An interoffice memo dated 10 September from *McCabe* co-producer David Foster to Warner Brothers executive Charles Greenlaw indicated the wide range of unusual location-related problems that this approach caused. The location had to be accepted and rezoned by the municipality of West Vancouver. In addition, Foster had received complaints from Warner Brothers concerning the expenditures Altman made to win the support for zoning. The director had included in his production budget reports rather sizable supermarket and liquor bills. Foster justified the "unusual expenses" in his memo as necessary public-relations expenditures. He explained to Greenlaw that "because of geographic locations" (and considering the relatively low, $3 million budget) it had become most feasible to establish a "restaurant-cocktail lounge" at the production house to entertain city leaders and landowners. Foster argued that their expenses were not excessive and were in fact the best means of accomplishing "what we set out to do," which was to secure the land and to procure a shipment of ore from the Anaconda Mines, with which they intended to color the landscape of Presbyterian Church. One month later Greenlaw responded to the memo, agreeing to the set-up but also telling Foster to be certain "that it *will* be handled properly."[3] Since Altman was already receiving the standard $750 weekly expense allowance from Warner Brothers, this letter was a warning to Foster to keep tight reins on the *McCabe* production. Greenlaw included in the letter a subtle threat to visit the location within a few weeks.

While all this was occurring, many changes in the screenplay were made, as Altman polished the dialogue and worked with Warren Beatty in writing revisions. The collaboration was not always easy. Beatty wanted to know where he stood from the beginning. He asked, for example, why he should enter a set in a prescribed manner; what the purpose of a particular camera set-up was; or what the viewer should learn from a specific conversation. These were insights that the director usually refrained from "spelling out" too specifically for his performers. While Altman found it difficult to work this way and he objected to Beatty's "nit-picking, with the way he pushed and bugged me," he also felt that Beatty "kept me honest."[4]

Three significant structural deviations from the screenplay are apparent in the film. First, the funeral of Bart Coyle is cross-cut with McCabe's trip to Bearpaw. This juxtaposition stresses the desperateness and hopelessness of his journey—qualities that were absent from the screenplay. Second, three scenes are eliminated between McCabe's first meeting with Mrs. Miller and his dinner with her. The deletion provided a more fluid transition for their tentative relationship. Finally, the ending of the film is modified to suggest a psychic and emotional bond between John McCabe and Constance Miller. This link was accomplished by cross-cutting close-ups of McCabe's frozen figure and of Mrs. Miller's dazed face.

Less significant changes in the narrative structure involved the rear-rangement of specific conversations and activities in Sheehan's bar in the beginning of the film. The exact moment of the Cowboy's arrival in Pres-byterian Church is changed, and some of the details of the chase scene between McCabe and the hired killers are deleted. Altman defined these changes as "stripping away a lot of plotty things." This desire to reduce the story to its barest elements continued during the editing. The final dele-tions pushed *McCabe* from a purely episodic structure to a series of inte-grated character sketches.

In particular, the alterations in dialogue from screenplay to screen en-hanced the sense of naturalism in the film. Sometimes an entire scene would be improvised based on an idea suggested in the screenplay. The birthday-party scene, for example, grew out of the verbal exchanges of the actresses. Most of McCabe's lines were changed by Warren Beatty. In one scene when McCabe straps on his holster and gun to hunt for the assas-sins, the screenplay calls for him to be "talking to himself, muttering something about 'poetry in my soul.'" From that kernel Beatty produced McCabe's final, eloquent monologue: "Well, I'll tell ya somethin', I got poetry in me. I do . . . she's freezin' my soul, nothing but a whore, but what the hell, [I] never was much of a percentage man. A whore's about the only kind of woman I could have."

The majority of Mrs. Miller's lines were read intact by Julie Christie, with the addition of a distinct Cockney accent. Background ad libs from other characters were also used, first being improvised by various actors in rehearsal, then added when their particular scene was filmed. Many of the less obvious alterations in the dialogue of the screenplay were essen-tially reductive. Conversations were shortened; other verbal exchanges among secondary characters were dropped solely because they drew the viewer's attention from John McCabe. Six pages of dialogue featuring the whores, Sheehan, and Gilchrist (Edwin Collier) were eliminated. Five pages of Sheehan's discussions with Quigley (Terrence Kelly), Smalley, and Joe Shortreed (Joe Clarke) disappeared. Numerous other brief con-versations with the townspeople and the Chinese workers were systemat-ically dropped from the script. *McCabe and Mrs. Miller* was no longer the crudely humorous morality play Altman had perhaps envisioned in 1960. Nor did it reflect the type of character portrait or western saga that Naughton, McKay, Beatty, or other cast members could suggest. Grad-ually the film evolved from those mixed sources into a study of a singular individual whose emotions, loves, and ideals were incompat-ible with the desires and fears of his friends, acquaintances, and compet-itors.

Altman desired a hazy visual quality for *McCabe and Mrs. Miller* in order "to complement the period, the set and the look of the people." Art director Leon Erickson and cinematographer Vilmos Zsigmond worked with Altman to achieve this effect. Soft colors were first selected for the sets. Then, to give the film a rusted-brown shade, ore was dumped on the location site. Zsigmond's use of fog filters throughout the shooting, except during the overexposed death scene of McCabe, further muted color contrast. Before the negative was developed, it was "flashed" or briefly exposed to light of different wavelengths. In this manner more blue and yellow were added to the print, giving it the appearance of a time-faded, bronze-tone photograph.

From August 1970 to June 1971 Altman and Louis Lombardo edited *McCabe and Mrs. Miller.* In a small sound studio at Starlight Equipment Rentals in North Vancouver the director began what he regarded as his "biggest problem" with the film. His approach to editing was a natural extension of his shooting style for *McCabe.* Since the film was shot in continuity, much unnecessary action had been eliminated during production. There were still many scenes, however, that needed to be cut because Altman thought "it was a long picture and I don't like long pictures." *McCabe* "demanded a style of editing that was not usual" for Altman. He also knew that the editing would not be a "fast cut" or an easy task. He "could not race it along because it has its own pace which is almost more important than what happens." This slow, careful process amplified the emotions of main characters, but it also diminished several characters and events already on the film's periphery. Still, Altman judged that most viewers would "sit back and accept the film," that they would "simply let the film wash over them."

Editing, of course, was only one of the chores that commanded the director's attention during this lengthy postproduction period. He worked to influence Warner Brothers' plans for the film's release, distribution, and publicity. He added the Leonard Cohen songs to the soundtrack. He grappled with the usual minor annoyances, such as the Writers Guild requirement for last-minute modification of Robert Altman's and Brian McKay's names on the writing credits.

With the date for the preview screening drawing nearer, postproduction problems seemed to multiply. The final remix of the film was nonetheless completed in early June. Since the editing had taken longer than Warner Brothers expected, two prints of the film had to be rushed from the Canadian lab to New York City. One of the prints contained an error in the optical soundtrack transfer from the master, and much of the dialogue was incomprehensible. The poor sound transfer, along with the use of overlapping dialogue, led critics to interpret the inaudibility as "calculated effrontery on the part of its director."[5]

Controversy over Leonard Cohen's Songs

Once this technical problem was resolved and Warner Brothers began general distribution on *McCabe and Mrs. Miller,* the film received high critical acclaim. A controversy focused, however, on the Leonard Cohen soundtrack, including "The Stranger Song," "Winter Lady," and "The Sisters of Mercy." Jan Dawson charged in *Sight and Sound* that the director was guilty of "extrapolating his scenario from the song,"[6] and Jackson Burgess in *Film Quarterly* objected to "the dismal fake ballad of Leonard Cohen."[7] Meanwhile, Pauline Kael admired "Leonard Cohen's lovely, fragile, ambiguous songs."[8]

The "quixotic" (Kael's term) interaction between the Cohen songs and the film characters deserves elucidation. The songs, with their enticingly appropriate connotations, seem intentionally misleading. "The Stranger Song" invites a depiction of John McCabe as a footloose drifter, leading a gambler's life and enjoying emphemeral relationships with women before moving to the next town.

The attitudes suggested in the song define an internal set of beliefs for McCabe that really does not match his character. The stranger is a background figure; McCabe enjoys the stories that are spreading about his "big rep." The stranger is completely independent; McCabe establishes a partnership with Constance Miller. The stranger is an enigma to the woman in song; McCabe is so transparent that Mrs. Miller can predict, "They'll get you, McCabe, they'll do somethin' terrible to you." There is an additional irony, since the viewer learns that McCabe is a man incapable of protecting himself. The stranger drifts in and out of relationships; McCabe assures Constance, "I'll be here, you don't have to worry."

On the other hand, there is a close fit between "Winter Lady"'s theme and Mrs. Miller's personality. "Winter Lady" captures Mrs. Miller's self-sufficiency and detachment. When McCabe says, "Now, now, ain't nothin' gonna happen to me, little lady," her response, "Don't give me any of that 'little lady' shit—I don't care about you," shows that she is "just a station on your way" and "not your lover."

Before the gunfight, however, their facades disappear. McCabe finally admits, "I never wanted to do nuthin' but put a smile on your face," and Mrs. Miller welcomes him to bed. For a moment the pretensions vanish. For a while, actions belie the lyrics of the songs. The moment passes quickly; their lives cannot be changed by this encounter. At dawn Mrs. Miller returns to her opium and John McCabe awaits assassination.

Since there is no single referent to conventional western characters and because there are subtle contradictions between the film narrative and the song lyrics, the viewer's perspective in *McCabe and Mrs. Miller* is quietly being challenged. The subliminal nature of the lyrics creates an uneasiness for the viewer. The songs are not simply descriptions of McCabe and Mrs. Miller, nor are they just counterpoints to the relationship the couple shares in the film. The Cohen songs are sophisticated and essential components of the process of characterization. They help Altman create an ambiguity that brings greater depth and complexity to the characters, and a fuller sense of irony and sadness to the film.

The Demise of the Western

McCabe and Mrs. Miller is an unusually complex and emotional western. The film is also a "revisionist look" at the West. Life is not easy for John McCabe in the imperfect world of Presbyterian Church. He tries to accommodate the wishes of Constance Miller and win her love and admiration—in the best of western traditions—but their relationship is always problematic. He tries to make a living as a small entrepreneur in a town that thrives on betrayals, dishonesty, greed, and affectations. All the inhabitants are seeking quick fortunes from the zinc mine, and no one is succeeding. In fact, no one except the Chinese coolies is ever seen working, and the mine itself appears inoperative. McCabe's associate Sheehan is a cowardly opportunist; his lawyer, Samuels, hopes to capitalize on McCabe's death. The town represents a reversal in the belief in the West as a second chance, a new Eden. While there is an admirable element of fortitude in John McCabe's struggle to survive, the general view of man in the film is as bleak as the one presented in the "anti-westerns" of Sam Peckinpah or Arthur Boetticher. Presbyterian Church is not the redemptive frontier that one finds in the films of John Ford and Howard Hawks. The obvious omission in Altman's depiction is the moral imperative, embodied by a lawman (in *My Darling Clementine*, for example) or by a man with an uncompromising moral code (in *Shane* or *The Searchers*). When the base of moral and legal jurisdiction shifted—or was divided between two individuals, as in *Red River*—some reconciliation and consequential realignment of audience sympathies always occurred.

The absence of law in Presbyterian Church permits the Harrison-Shaugnessy Company to operate with a free hand, and it also sanctions murder. The close-up on the body of the young cowboy (Keith Carradine) in the frozen stream, after he is shot by the Kid (Manfred Shultz), foreshadows McCabe's death in the snow, but it also reveals that murders such as this one occur without demand for retribution. McCabe comes closest to a figure of moral authority in the film. He may be ironically viewed as an unwitting agent of reform; but his pursuit of the assassins is not motivated by outrage or by a need for revenge for the death of the cowboy. McCabe instead acts out of self-defense. He supports "bustin' up monopolies" only to stay alive. He also hopes that his action will be interpreted by his associates as a case of the "little man standing up to the big organization." His death, unfortunately, goes unnoticed. Samuels, the Bearpaw lawyer, clearly exemplifies the hopeless state of legal recourse on the western frontier. The inversion of names, from Samuel Clemens to Clem Samuels, suggests the perversion of American romanticism and the impossibility of finding a retreat from the material traps of civilization. Falling back upon his stereotypic notion of law enforcement, McCabe alludes to the need for a marshal. Samuels's quick rejection of this approach reveals his personal motivation in the case and the influence the Harrison-Shaugnessy Company has upon him. His answer further suggests that mediation by a marshal would be impossible, improper, and ineffectual.

The major cause of this deterioration of the mythic West, as depicted in *McCabe and Mrs. Miller*, is the influence of large businesses. The film argues that the greed with which corporations such as Harrison-Shaugnessy divided the riches of the West resulted in the complete loss of individual freedom. When McCabe mentions Harrison-Shaugnessy, Mrs. Miller immediately says, "zinc," recognizing the monopolistic identity of the company and the extent of its control. And even though McCabe states, " 'Course I know who they are," he obviously has a poor understanding of Harrison-Shaugnessy's power and ruthlessness; he regards Mrs. Miller's assertion that "they'd as soon put a bullet in your back as look at you" as hyperbole. The film thus works contrary to the conventional western ideology by asserting that corrupt and self-serving large companies actually controlled the destiny of the American frontier.

The lively sense of humor displayed in *McCabe and Mrs. Miller* helps keep the film from brooding over this somber state of affairs. The film's humor derives from the affectations and clichés John McCabe uses to impress Mrs. Miller, and from its broader satires on western life and accepted beliefs.

McCabe entertains himself and the patrons of Sheehan's bar with a number of comic gestures and jokes that fall flat when performed in Mrs. Miller's company. The first time McCabe drinks a raw egg in his whiskey he wins the admiration of the Sheehan crowd. When he later tries the same routine on Mrs. Miller he draws a blank stare. His joke about a frog and his sarcastic remarks about Sheehan earn hearty laughs in the bar. When he comments that Mrs. Miller probably will "eat a horse" at Sheehan's, she labels him as "another frontier wit." His speech is filled with clichés, especially apparent in his conversations with Sears and Hollander: like Mrs. Miller they conclude that "he's a real smart ass" and "just plain impossible." His idiosyncrasies and jokes work well when McCabe is performing for his intellectual inferiors. His attempts to use the same material on peers ironically make him appear as one of Sheehan's barroom buffoons.

McCabe's professional and romantic ties with Mrs. Miller provide another source of comic relief. After bathing and changing clothes, with flowers in hand he courts Mrs. Miller, only to address her through a closed door and to pay for her services. When he is told by Mrs. Miller that he was not capable of running a profitable, large sporting house by himself, he tries to prove the opposite by balancing the books. He is baffled by her talk of "debit columns" and "credits" and by her quiz (i.e., "What's fourteen from twenty-three?"). McCabe boasts, "I can hold my own in any game of chance with any amount you can count . . . so don't give me any horse-pucky 'cause it takes me a little time to write it down formal." His rationale is childish; still, his attempt to bluff her concerning his talent and ability is painfully amusing.

Satire in the film centers on the contrast between the townspeople, who drink, argue, and fight for the majority of the film, and Mrs. Miller's prostitutes, who are convivial and helpful with each other. The sporting house is a clean and efficient operation. Its mistress communicates a deep personal concern for the health and happiness of each of her girls; Mrs. Miller resembles Flora, the madame of the Bear Flag restaurant in Steinbeck's *Cannery Row*. The prostitutes display the only real sense of community in the film. They are present at the Coyle funeral, and compassion is evident in their attempt to save the church when it catches fire.

Their concern for one another certainly underscores the general disregard for life shared by the other inhabitants. While the girls comfort Ida Coyle, Sheehan describes with enthusiasm the new plan to send coolies into the already unstable mine tunnels with dynamite to explore for additional zinc deposits. The men in the bar unanimously and without second thought welcome that procedure as an effective, laudable idea. The very basis of McCabe's appeal in Presbyterian Church is that he killed a man; murder is respectable. John McCabe's denials of having shot Bill Rountree are politely accepted as indications of McCabe's modesty. The minister Elliott condones violence. He blasts McCabe with his shotgun to stop him from entering his church. The dark irony of *McCabe and Mrs. Miller* functions as an indictment of casual attitudes toward life in the West.

Altman's characterizations expressed through Beatty's and Christie's performances are open-ended and captivating. The viewer deduces causal relationships, weighs the relevance of peripheral information, and estimates the plausibility of character actions. This process, however, demands active participation, and it decreases emotional involvement with the characters at times. Mrs. Miller's most puzzling quality, for example, is her opium addiction. The viewer may guess at some rationale for the habit, or may make the stereotypic association of opium with moral degeneracy. In both cases, empathy with Mrs. Miller considerably diminishes. The viewer has an equally difficult time evaluating McCabe's character.

His insights about the power and influence of the mining company are sophomoric. He calmly explains that "there comes a time in every man's life, Constance, when a man must put his hand in the fire and see what he's made of." This new philosophy is shocking, and it is either indicative of a desperate man taken in by his own reputation or reflects a genuine heroic stance. The first alternative defines McCabe as a completely pathetic figure; the second is contrary to the systematic removal of McCabe from heroic stature throughout the film. These aspects of characterization limit the degree to which the viewer can appreciate and share the fragile sentiments and elusive passions of John McCabe and Constance Miller.

Although characterization is atypical, some elements in *McCabe and Mrs. Miller* resemble noteworthy examples of the genre. There are obviously no conscious homages, but the similarities are striking. For instance, *McCabe and Mrs. Miller* parallels *The Gold Rush* in the actions and appearances of the protagonists. McCabe rides into town wearing a bowler hat and a huge bearskin coat. His movements are fluid and easy, yet he is completely out of place in Presbyterian Church. He looks like the Lone Prospector strolling through the snow to his camp in *The Gold Rush*. The eccentricities of the character provide excellent barroom entertainment for the miners. Both men fall in love with beautiful women of questionable honor; both films are set at approximately the same time and place; and both films illustrate the difficult struggle to establish order and sensibility in hostile environments.

The winning of the West many times took a back seat to romance. The fact that the woman may be a prostitute is not unique to *McCabe and Mrs. Miller*. Henry Hathaway's *North to Alaska* portrays the love and conflicts between Sam McCord and the French whore Angel. *Two Mules for Sister Sarah* also documents a loner's relationship with a prostitute: in this film Sarah is disguised as a nun. Each of these films analyzes hypocritical attitudes toward life, love, and religion prevalent in the West at the turn of the century.

Relatively few westerns, however, were made after *McCabe*, just as there were few television westerns after *Bonanza*. Although westerns with disparaging themes or with antiheroes *(Hombre, Fistful of Dollars, Once Upon a Time in the West)* and parodies of westerns *(Support Your Local Sheriff, Cat Ballou)* had been popular for quite some time, Altman dealt the coup de grace to the traditional concept of the genre. Directors would avoid the old plots and themes unless they were safely hidden in another genre *(Assault on Precinct 13, Smokey and the Bandit, Outland, The Man from Snowy River)*. With *McCabe and Mrs. Miller* and *Buffalo Bill and the Indians*, Altman contributed not to the decline but to the demise of the western.

McCabe and Mrs. Miller is really a story without traditional heroes and villains, no matter how strongly the viewer may yearn for such traditional type. Superficial heroes abound in *Buffalo Bill and the Indians*. Legend becomes fact at the Wild West show on a day-to-day basis there, but *McCabe and Mrs. Miller* denies the legend and shows only some of the facts. There are so many epic conversations, lectures, and sermons in *Buffalo Bill and the Indians* that there is hardly any time for action. The main ideas in *McCabe*, on the other hand, are understated and its actions are as antiheroic as its words. In 1971 *McCabe and Mrs. Miller* was Robert Altman's best film; along with *Nashville*, it is one of his most effective.

5

Images

IN THE FINAL SCENE OF *McCabe and Mrs. Miller,* Constance Miller's face dissolves in diffracted images, suggesting her confused thoughts on the loss of John McCabe. Robert Altman begins *Images* where *McCabe* ends, establishing Cathryn Ryder (Susannah York) as being equally trapped by her emotions and by memories of her husband, with her fragmented state of consciousness represented by a glass mobile hanging from a window in the foreground.

In Tennessee Williams's *The Glass Menagerie,* the objects that surround Laura Wingfield represent her physical frailty. In *Images,* the mobiles, camera lenses, mirrors, windows, and windshields do not suggest this kind of weakness. The viewer is informed that there is "nothing wrong, physically" with Cathryn, who at first glance seems to possess the same sturdiness of many Altman female protagonists, including Mrs. Wade in *The Long Goodbye,* Willie in *Three Women,* and the Vivia in *Quintet.* The reflective objects in *Images* are indicative of Cathryn's complex and troubled personality and they also suggest an intermixing of illusion and reality. Cathryn is motivated by opposing drives that shatter her grasp of reality. She feels guilty about her past extramarital affairs and about her secret desires to relive those assignations. Her fantasies of past lovers, her defensive denial of those affairs, the projection of similar desires onto her husband, and her abnormally close identification with a young girl are symptomatic of a psychological malaise building within Cathryn. On one level, *Images* tells the story of an unfortunate individual's deterioration into a specific form of paranoid schizophrenia.

The analysis of self-image and self-perception in *Images,* however, is quite confusing. The already-complicated personality of Cathryn is hidden within obscure visual riddles, engimas, conflicts, and subplots. Cathryn remains virtually unknowable. She battles intermittently with hallucinations, and Altman provides no information about the source of the hallucinations or where her visions begin and end. Altman assumes an omnisicient, noncommittal position toward Cathryn. He refrains from judging her. Instead, he depicts each unique thought and action of hers,

Cathryn (Susannah York) tries to ignore her hallucination of Marcel (Hugh Millais) in Images. *Courtesy of University of Wisconsin (Madison) State Archives.*

intending for the viewer to acquire an intense, emotional understanding of her life. But before unlocking these mysteries, the viewer must sort through gaps in the narrative of the film and through an ambiguous thematic structure. The task quickly becomes tedious.

Images is in many ways the study of a character in a vacuum. Very few parts of Cathryn's peculiar existence are relevant to society. The main characters are nonindigenous to American culture and seem at odds with the Irish setting of the film. The film probes the condition of madness, but more importantly it examines an isolated consciousness. The social pressures that often drive other Altman characters to desperate actions are categorically absent from Images; all the pressures working on Cathryn are internally derived. In creating this psychodrama the director has abandoned one of his fortes—the investigation and dissection of American society and culture. Often in Altman films, solitary characters (e.g., Bowie Bowers in Thieves Like Us and Charlie Waters in California Split) suffer because of their psychological quirks. But in each instance their fate is pretty much decided by their rejection of a restrictive society, and by their own battle with an antagonistic universe. On the other hand, Cathryn's masochism results from fundamental self-deceptions—Cathryn lacks an ability to view herself honestly. Worse, she possesses few, if any, saving graces. Her dual role as victim and torturer and her sadistic delight in extremes of real and imagined violence are morally repugnant.

Images is thus an unusual Altman work because of its theme and because of its style. It is a much more exacting, meticulous, and controlled film than Brewster McCloud or McCabe. These very qualities seem to restrain Altman's typically "instinctive" style. Much of the dialogue is found verbatim in the screenplay—which was written by Altman over a period of five years. The only substantial addition through eight revisions of that screenplay was a voice-over narration by Susannah York. Another element at odds with the Altman "trademarks" is the casting. The performances work against Altman's ideas for the various roles in the film.

The conflicting desires of the director are central problems in Images. Altman wanted a film that was simultaneously detached and emotional. He regarded the protagonist's problems as unique but also as universally intelligible. Thus the tone of the film is often contradictory. At times it seems to incorporate elements of the gothic-horror tradition (the interior sets of the apartment and the cottage) and the murder-mystery genre (the presence of the "other," diabolical Cathryn). At other times it resembles a film of sentiment (her arguments and reconciliation with Hugh) and a fairy tale (the In Search of Unicorns characters). This irresoluteness marks Images as an ambiguous and problematic work.

Altman sets the story of such personal and psychological magnitude within a relatively simple plot. Plagued by her own hallucinations of past lovers, Cathryn and her husband, Hugh (René Auberjonois), who is unaware of the nature of her problem, decided to vacation at their country home. Cathryn's hallucinations increase in number and severity, and soon she accepts those images as reality. She takes drastic and violent steps to rid herself of the visions that trouble her. Mistaking Hugh for one of her own hallucinations, she kills him. Thinking herself cured by that action, she returns to their city home. There she finds herself trapped in a private hell of her obsessions, hallucinations, and rampant and perpetual fears.

Production History

The story, the economical settings, and the small cast suggest obvious limitations on the director's freedom in preproduction and shooting. The production history of *Images* indicates that some of these limitations were self-imposed, while others resulted from the small budget with which Altman was working. Altman felt that he needed a nonspecific location, a setting that did not identify a particular culture. In his first draft of the screenplay he called for a seashore in Big Sur or in Vancouver or in Maine. The increased cost of filming in British Columbia forced him to forsake the Vancouver site. When Hollywood studios rejected the script, which called for the on-location shooting in California or Maine, Altman decided to produce the film independently through Lion's Gate, and he spent a year scouting locations in Europe. He needed close proximity to a studio in the same vicinity as the exteriors. Unable to locate a suitable spot in France, Greece, Spain, Sweden, or England, he and producer Tommy Thompson discovered a setting in Ireland near the Ardmore Studios in Bray, just south of Dublin. The studio, which had gone into receivership, was willing to accommodate Altman's crew. Production began on 28 October 1971, and finished on 19 December of that year.

With the cooperation of London's Hemdale Group, Ltd., Altman produced the film on a budget of slightly over $800,000. Most external shooting was done near Loch Bray, but the director also did location shooting at as many sites around Dublin as his budget would permit. Cast and crew members assisted the director in his struggle with finances. His performers worked for lower salaries. Vilmos Zsigmond accepted a cut in salary to work again as Altman's cinematographer, and Zsigmond's assistant cameraman, Earl Clarke, took almost a 50 percent salary cut from his *Deliverance* salary. Leon Erickson economically simulated plush, "expensive" apartment sets and remote, rustic, cabin interiors. Editor Graeme Clifford suggested scoring the film with wind chimes—an economical move which, along with the music composed by John Williams, added an ethereal quality to many of the scenes.

The complexities of *Images* originate in the detailed screenplay by Altman. He worked with the idea that "a person will set up a false jealousy of their partner in order to justify their own infidelity. Then I got the idea of mixing up images and the fright in that."[1] Altman began writing in London in 1967 and continued in Santa Barbara "three months, thirty pages later,"[2] several years before he began *M*A*S*H*. The eighty-page treatment, which he typed and revised by hand on note paper, reveals most of the ideas and actions of *Images* in their barest form. Kathryn's husband is Steve; her deceased lover is Vince; and the "other man" is Wayne. The names later changed to Hugh, René, and Marcel. Altman assigned the actor's first name to one of the other leads in the film once it was cast. Hugh Millais, who played Dog Butler in *McCabe and Mrs. Miller,* was called Marcel. Marcel Bozzuffi was the dead lover, René. René Auberjonois played Cathryn's husband, Hugh. The spelling of "Kathryn" changed to "Cathryn" with the casting of Cathryn Harrison as Susannah, who was Cathryn's young girlfriend and the daughter of Marcel in the film. The name switching served no function in the film and few viewers even noticed the switch. Playing with names, then, is one example of the lack of conceptual thoroughness in *Images*.

In the rough draft and the first few revisions of *Images*, the narrative and themes of the film were explicit. Beginnings and ends of hallucinations were clearly delineated. The identities of each of the men, and their relationships to "Kathryn," were immediately evident. In the film, however, the characters' motivations, and the events that lead to Cathryn's hallucinations, are less clear. In the rough drafts there is a dinner scene in which Kathryn discusses with her husband her problem distinguishing between illusion and reality. Later she sees Steve sitting at the table, but she hears Vince talking to her about her "false jealousy": "Maybe you've been mixed up all these years . . . suppose it was really *me* you were married to and it was *him* that was killed in the plane crash." Altman retained those lines through the revisions of the screenplay, but cut them from the film because they were too pedantic.

Marital tensions, which are only implied in the film, are developed at length in the script. On one occasion, Steve hears Kathryn yelling, "Shut up!" Unaware that she is talking to Vince, Steve turns to his wife, asking, "Who was that meant for, Kathryn—who were you saying 'shut up' to?" After Kathryn says she was just talking to herself, Steve remarks that he finds that odd. Kathryn replies, "What the hell's the difference. Big deal. So I said 'shut up.' Does that mean I'm crazy?" Switching the subject, Steve asks, "Do you know how long it's been since we've made love?" and Kathryn yells, "Oh, God. Don't start that now." The conversation points to specific problems in their relationship, and suggests that Kathryn is escaping an unpleasant marriage through her hallucinations. The exchange was eliminated from the film—an economical but ambiguous revision. This process of refinement through reduction is also evident in the on-screen characterizations of Hugh and Cathryn. In the second revision of the screenplay, Kathryn's husband tells her, "I don't know what it is you want, but whatever it is, it's getting pretty clear that I can't give it to you." The film never endows Hugh with this sense of frustration.

In the various script revisions Kathryn attempts suicide, slashing her wrists with the broken stems of two wineglasses. In the film she breaks the glasses but does not attempt to injure herself. Altman carefully avoids the physical manifestations of her masochism; rather, psychological horrors predominate.

Altman attempted to supplement these abridgments of the screenplay by encouraging input from his performers. When he wanted a scene that would reveal the relationship between the woman and the girl, Altman told Susannah York, "You'll work it out—do whatever you wanna do—you're supposed to be the big inventive actress." She improvised one of the few relaxed scenes in *Images*, in which she and Susannah play with a jigsaw puzzle. Later, she allowed Altman to use the text of the children's book that she had previously written, called *In Search of Unicorns*, as an intricate part of the divided personality of Cathryn. Apart from these two individual contributions, Susannah York closely followed the script for Cathryn. She changed idiomatic expressions and altered words for more comfortable readings, as did Auberjonois, Millais, and Bozzuffi. But critics' assertions that the actors rewrote a substantial part of the dialogue do not bear up under close examination of the script. They enlivened their respective roles, but never exceeded the limitations outlined in the script or challenged the philosophy of deliberate understatement in *Images*.

Problems with Characterization

Strict adherence to script was unusual for Altman. Also, the only other film script Altman wrote and revised, without the assistance of another screenwriter, was *Three Women*. Both films have sketchy plots, vague themes, and uneasy symbolism, indicating perhaps that Altman works better with a collaborator, and best with a good collaborator, like Leigh Brackett or Joan Tewkesbury. *Images* feels too tightly wound, too meticulous, and this is due largely to the fact that its script was subjected to five years—rather than just two or three months—of revision and deletions by the director. This suggests further that Altman writes better when he writes quickly, as was the case in *The Long Goodbye*, *Thieves Like Us*, *California Split*, and *A Wedding*. During lengthy rewrites, Altman was so familiar with his concepts that he expected others to grasp the meaning without many clues. Apparently the director hoped that the personalities of the characters would become more evident to the viewer if the roles were cast properly. A serious problem with *Images*, however, lies in the discrepancies between what he had attempted in casting[3] and the characterizations that were presented onscreen. For example, Altman hoped that René Auberjonois would be perceived as a "very unattractive man." He believed that Auberjonois would best be able "to get off into a kind of effeminate thing." He knew of "very few actors who would expose themselves that much, on that level" as the "very boring, straight" husband, insensitive to Cathryn's needs.

Auberjonois's portrayal of Hugh is most effective for exactly opposite reasons. Hugh is the only strong, intelligent figure in the film. He is the only person with any control over Cathryn. Despite a penchant for poor jokes, he is calm, rational, and forceful. Though sometimes manipulated by his wife, Hugh's resourcefulness and his total concern for her well-being make him a very attractive figure in times of crisis. During his daily routine he appears compassionate and very human, whether he is patiently explaining to Cathryn his sudden need to return to the city or helping her prepare dinner. His sexual vigor is evident in his mood and conversation the morning after Cathryn's imagined orgy. There is no visual evidence of effeminacy. Had Auberjonois suggested the questionable sexual identity Altman had planned, Cathryn's affairs and her need to reexperience their excitement would seem more comprehensible. The viewer would very likely applaud her infidelity as a normal reaction to an unfulfilling sexual relationship. Her feelings of guilt would be undercut, and her projections of jealousy would appear ridiculous. Cathryn was unfaithful to Hugh, but his moral, intellectual, and emotional superiority quickly separates him from a stereotypic cuckold.

Tragedy in *Images* depends, to a large extent, on the death of the innocent husband. The feeling of dread that overwhelms Cathryn when she suspects that she killed Hugh would lose its significance for the viewer if one felt ambivalence toward him. His death would simply have been an unfortunate consequence of Cathryn's insanity. Auberjonois was not consciously subverting Altman's direction. Rather, given the truly unattractive natures of the other characters in the film, Hugh naturally emerged as the sole object of viewer sympathy.

At the other extreme, Altman saw in René "the supreme lover" with "a Charles Boyer continental thing." He believed Marcel Bozzuffi embodied those qualities. He thought Bozzuffi was "extremely attractive" and masculine, and had "a fantastic kind of smile." Bozzuffi (whose English is indecipherable throughout most of the film) is credible as René only because he is so unattractive. He is, in essence, a mouthpiece for Cathryn, for the unpleasant part of her personality, which wants to live only in the past. He has no life independent of her memories. René represents a low point in her life. He mumbles clichés, makes lewd remarks, and is told by Cathryn that he has a "filthy mind." He exhibits qualities inappropriate for an "extremely attractive" male lead. According to Cathryn, he has acceded to her every whim: hiding in public so that she will not be embarrassed; allowing himself to be used emotionally and sexually; and even volunteering his own death. As the third party to a love triangle, René has few positive features to assuage that disapprobation. No matter what "kind of smile" Bozzuffi possesses, René cannot be accepted as a strong or attractive figure.

Since he is the unwelcomed projection of Cathryn's torn mind, when René is shot, the viewer is relieved that his ghost will no longer bother her. Unfortunately, she still must face her friend Marcel. His unshaved appearance, his uncouth behavior, and his lack of understanding of Cathryn and of his own daughter make him no more likable than René. As the attractiveness of Hugh's competitors decreases, the viewer's sympathy for Hugh naturally grows.

Altman's decision to cast Susannah York as Cathryn, instead of Julie Christie, Sandy Dennis, or Vanessa Redgrave, was made while he was flying to Europe to scout locations for the film. He saw her starring in *Jane Eyre*, the in-flight movie, and was at once "intrigued" by her appearance. She seemed to offer the perfect solution to the problem; Altman was trying to find a woman whose mere attractiveness would be sufficient to prevent the viewer from being bored with her. The seven preliminary drafts of the *Images* script also indicated that Altman regarded the role of Cathryn as undemanding, requiring only a pretty, if troubled, face.

In truth, the role of Cathryn is impossibly complicated. She is at once an inscrutable psychopath and a pitiable victim; an obsessed murderer and her own torturer; a woman coexisting in fantasy and fact. Cathryn is a living contradiction. She desires to relive past affairs, and to continue more recent excitements with Marcel, but her feelings of guilt are too great to permit more than momentary dreams. Her sudden transformation from a victim to a hellion—hitting René with an ashtray, shooting him, stabbing Marcel, and pushing Hugh over a cliff—seems most implausible. Susannah York effectively communicated Cathryn's timidity, vulnerability, and fear. Her rage and her temper tantrums do not fit the soft-spoken qualities that York favored.

Cathryn is always nervous; she relaxes momentarily in Susannah's presence, but cannot completely overcome her emotional edginess. Her lapses into sarcasm represent a further inconsistency in her otherwise fragile character. Her dialogue betrays the gravity of the situation. After wounding René, she mocks the apparition, saying, "My, the ghost bleeds." She

takes a sadistic delight in plotting the death of Marcel. When Marcel tells
her, "I understand you," she replies, "Oh, yeah?," while she hides a pair
of long-pointed scissors behind her arm. This problem of appropriateness
of characterization for Cathryn may have resulted from Altman's search to
find some specific acts for her to perform while she was going mad, acts
that would move the narrative and would show her at the edge of sanity.
He assumed that he "couldn't have her just sitting around waiting for odd
things to happen." For those activities, however, Altman included far too
many scenes depicting Cathryn in motion: jumping around the house,
running through a forest, driving her car, or reciting parts of *In Search of
Unicorns* while walking. The scenes suggest her need for escape, but they
also result in a noticeable aimlessness in her character. Besides being repetitious, this meandering makes her moods appear even more erratic,
since at one moment she is calmly talking to herself at a waterfall in the
woods and in the next she sees herself fighting with Marcel. This constant
movement and shifting of scenes make Cathryn unattractive to the viewer.

Interestingly, Altman worried "how aware the audience is going to be
that this [Cathryn's behavior] is a problem of schizophrenia." His concern
is odd, since the film constantly and blatantly defines Cathryn as mentally
ill. On one occasion Cathryn tells Marcel, "I've been sick, I am sick," to
which he responds, "You're a schizo—one minute you're fighting like a
tiger, and the next, all love and kisses." René tells her that Hugh will
"think you are crazy if he comes in and hears you talking to yourself." In
spite of Hugh's assurance that "there's no one else, there is only you, just
you," she still feels the presence of an intruding entity, of her own divided
identity. In the beginning of the film, she has a lengthy, frightening telephone conversation with herself, during which she keeps screaming,
"Who is this?" Each room in that house is filled with mirrors and reflected
images. In her hallucinations she sees herself as two women, one wearing
a white coat and the other a black one.

In the fantasy world of *Unicorns* she writes about the creatures called
Ums, and she endows them with all the conflicts of her own personality.
They are "quarrelsome, peaceful; jealous, kind; cowardly, brave; happy
and sad." Altman's decision to use this story, in a voice-over narration by
Cathryn, draws additional attention to her psychological problems. This
overdetermination causes problems throughout the film. For example,
many times Cathryn pleads with herself: "Go away," "I don't want to see
you," "Go back," and "I can't hear you." She sees her naked body reclining
in bed, with a smile on her face. Cathryn is shown losing the ability to
separate herself from the creatures in her visions. Her incipient loss of this
perspective marks the difference between sanity and insanity and con-
demns Cathryn to a nightmarish world of wild fantasies and appalling
memories. Any fears of Altman's, that Cathryn's schizophrenia would go

unnoticed, therefore, seem inappropriate. Altman included the numerous references to the private thoughts of Cathryn to sketch a detailed picture of schizophrenia.

He believed *Images* should "work on the audiences's emotions, not give them an intellectual exercise." A purely emotional involvement is impossible, however, given the conflicting versions of reality that the viewer has to manage. The fact that René's words belong to Cathryn and that his sole purpose in *Images* is to express her intimate thoughts and wishes is one example of affective confusion in the film. Unfortunately, then, there are crucial differences between the audience's perception of the film and what the director believed he had captured.

The extensive and uncontrolled use of symbolism in *Images* further obfuscates the characterization of Cathryn. The bedroom and bathroom walls are lined with mirrors. The Green Cove cottage, which is Cathryn and Hugh's pastoral retreat, is made into a prison with double sets of doors, walk-in closets, and narrow hallways. A swinging door in the kitchen suggests her rapid shifts from reality to illusion. Even her drive home from Green Cove is an ordeal; she is caught in a blur of neon lights, colors, and memories. The use of these symbols and the presence of cameras, lenses, and binoculars in the cottage make her actions seem more ambiguous and mysterious than they probably are. The repeated use of reflective symbols indicates the extent to which Altman was willing to engage the viewer in a distracting and complex set of visual metonymic codes.

The soundtrack of the film is also supposed to indicate her divided nature. Sound alternates between melodic compositions and intrusions of the strange sound effects by Stormu Yamashta—which are preludes to the point-of-view shots of her hallucinations. The device is too difficult to recognize given the ambiguous nature of the visuals.

Symbolic cinematographic and editing patterns are employed in the film, with varying degrees of success. For example, the cinematography of the night driving sequence resembles scenes in *That Cold Day,* and in Martin Scorsese's *Taxi Driver,* where characters operate in a world of "surrealistic fantasy and moral indefiniteness."[4] Cathryn is twice framed against backgrounds of blinding white light (in allusions to *Persona*), and this does enhance the foreboding nature of her actions. The director also pans the camera with her in profile on numerous occasions. This has a plausible synechdochic function, reiterating the fact that she keeps part of herself hidden from the observations of others at all times. Altman uses three dissolves in *Images* to provide links between Cathryn's delusions and her shrinking perception of reality, but the technique still does not help very much to clarify the problem Altman has created for the viewer with this characterization.

The camerawork is certainly very controlled: the camera always approaches Cathryn in a detached, voyeuristic manner, suggesting her own feeling of being watched. Cathryn is framed, for example, standing in the kitchen, only visible if one's gaze is focused first through a hallway, then through an empty room, and then through a window in the kitchen wall. Along with the shots of cameras and mirrors, scenes such as this one are indices of her paranoia, communicating at least an atmosphere of constant surveillance and examination. This rigorous framing culminates in a brief scene in which Cathryn looks into the viewfinder of a camera. In the background of the shot Hugh is visible, observing Cathryn through a window and a hallway. Here Altman has captured (in too complex a manner) a linear visual regression, with Hugh watching Cathryn look through a camera. She later destroys the camera, but her fears of being observed remain quite strong. She even spectates, and when she sees herself in bed with Hugh, her perception and pleasures are those of a voyeur.

Thus critics tended to judge the film as an outright "conceptual failure"[5] and "claustrophobic," contending that it should have "open[ed] into the landscape of the mind which the subject promises."[6] Actually, the film does not deserve such sweeping criticism. If Altman aimed too high with *Images*, he never "promised" that the film would be wide open or that it would be a universal mental landscape. *Images* is a very subjective film, with confusing themes and peripatetic techniques. But there are moments of brilliant visual insight as well. The intense hatred of René, the love and dependency between Cathryn and Susannah, the realization of the murder of Hugh—these are the fleeting moments that redeem the film, that make it a rewarding and significant film experience.

Altman continued to choose unlikely situations for his films, such as an ice age in *Quintet* or a health-food convention in *Health*. He again employed ambiguous thematic structures, evident in the diary entries and dream sequences of *Three Women*. He again mixed fantasy and reality, in a more sophisticated manner, in *Buffalo Bill and the Indians*. But after *Images* (with the sole exception of *Quintet*) Robert Altman did not produce or direct films that lacked references to significant social, political, or economic problems in America. He never again handcuffed himself with the serious problems of psychological characterization as is the unfortunate case in *Images*.

6

Genre and Popular Culture Films

ROBERT ALTMAN QUICKLY RETURNED to the United States after completing the postproduction work on *Images* and he began reviewing novels and scripts for future projects. His choice of source material for his next three films (an adaptation of a Raymond Chandler novel, a story of gangsters during the Depression, and a "hip" treatment of gambling) indicates that Altman desired projects that would appeal to larger audiences than *Images* had—subjects through which he could also comment on widespread, moral hypocrisy in America.

The Long Goodbye

Altman was approached by Jerry Bick and Elliott Kastner of United Artists to direct a treatment of *The Long Goodbye*. When Altman accepted the offer, Leigh Brackett, who was experienced in the genre and who had collaborated with Faulkner and Furthman on *The Big Sleep*, had completed her first draft of the script. She took a few liberties with the Chandler novel. The role of Harlan Potter, Sylvia Lennox's rich father, was eliminated, and Roger Wade's murder was changed to a suicide. Also, Brackett has Marlowe murder Terry Lennox.

After discussing her treatment of the novel with Altman, she began to streamline the story. According to the director, Brackett was very cooperative in this undertaking—"she had no ego about changing the scenes. She was very professional, very good for us. [I] added a few characters, introduced a situation or two, made a couple of connections, but there were no great changes."[1] The first draft was very close to the finished film. Once the revision was complete, Altman took charge of the project, retaining Brackett as an advisor, to help with later dialogue changes.

Altman instructed the entire cast to read *Raymond Chandler Speaking*, a collection of letters in which Chandler described his concept of the private detective. Altman and Brackett then convinced a skeptical United

Same actor, different genres: top, *Elliott Gould (Philip Marlowe) with Mark Rydell (Marty Augustine) in* The Long Goodbye. *Courtesy of United Artists, New York, NY;* bottom, *Gould (Charlie) watches George Segal (Bill) roll the dice in* California Split. *Courtesy of Films Incorporated, Wilmette, IL.*

61

Artists that Elliott Gould, who had been in contact with Altman during the filming of *McCabe and Mrs. Miller*, was the ideal choice for the role of Philip Marlowe. Production began on June 15, 1972. *The Long Goodbye* was Altman's first Hollywood project since *M*A*S*H*. But it was far from a typical Hollywood production. His nonconformity was evident in his use of little-known actors, his method of shooting in sequence, his penchant for location shooting, his unfaltering trust in his advisors and actors, and his small budgets. The film was shot on backlots, on-location in Hollywood and Los Angeles, and at Altman's home in the Malibu Colony. Cast members, especially Gould, wrote additional dialogue in rehearsals, with the assistance and encouragement of Brackett and Altman. The performers' own idiosyncrasies, such as the talents of a Malibu security guard for impersonating movie stars, were often incorporated into the roles and retained in the film. Production was completed on August 24 after eight weeks of shooting.

As a product of the collaboration of Altman, Brackett, and Gould, the character of Philip Marlowe is noticeably different from earlier literary and cinematic incarnations of the Chandler hero. It is updated to the 1970s in many ways. Marlowe stops quoting T. S. Eliot and drinking vodka gimlets and begins playing with cats and ordering "Canadian Club and ginger ale." By supressing Marlowe's intellectuality, Altman and Brackett encourage the viewer to regard Marlowe as another "dumb guy," "a cheapie," "a nickel's worth of nothing." He lives in a cluttered apartment: even gangster Marty Augustine (Mark Rydell) complains to Marlowe, "You keep your heart in an ashcan."

The 1970s version of Marlowe presents the detective as seemingly out of touch with his world. He even drives a 1948 Lincoln Continental. His emotions seem naive and repressed, especially in his loyalty to his buddy Terry Lennox (Jim Bouton), who lies to him and uses him. The first time the audience is aware of Marlowe's contemporary sensibility is when he shoots Terry. Then it becomes clear that Marlowe has been able to navigate his way through the maze of deceptions, threats, and murders because he is smart. His favorite remark, "It's okay with me," is not just an expression of apathy or complacency, as it is for Bowie in *Thieves Like Us*, for Charlie in *California Split*, or for the crowd in the end of *Nashville*. "It's okay with me" is a delaying tactic, allowing Marlowe to refrain from acting until he accumulates more complete knowledge about a subject. It is also a defense mechanism he uses to cover up feelings of outrage and helplessness.

The dialogue is inspired and right on target; Gould enhances the caustic wit of Chandler's Marlowe with his loose delivery. He sarcastically gives his agenda for the day to the hood Harry (David Arkin), assigned to follow him, just in case Harry is delayed in traffic. In a scene with a detective

Altman establishes the complex mise-en-scène of the Wade home scene, with Elliott Gould and Nina Van Pallandt in The Long Goodbye. *Courtesy of the Museum of Modern Art, New York, NY.*

investigating the death of Terry Lennox, Marlowe quips, "This is where I say, 'What's all this about?' and you say, 'We ask the questions.'" The patter with Marty Augustine is equally hardboiled. Marlowe wisecracks, "I only see hoods by appointment." An annoyed Augustine smashes a Coca-Cola bottle in his girlfriend's face, turns to Marlowe, and says, "Now that is somebody I love. You, I don't even like."

Humor also results from Marlowe's personal eccentricities. His whimsical interactions with his cat indicate a warm and human side to the loner. Those references to his cat and his similar involvement with Lennox suggest a code of honor that Marlowe upholds in a void, since the cat disappears and Lennox betrays him. His appearance never changes except when his clothes are taken from him in the hospital room—Altman joked that "Marlowe's idea of getting dressed up would be to put on a clean shirt with the same suit and tie."

Marlowe always seems a few steps behind the action in *The Long Goodbye.* The police unravel many of the complexities of the case while he sits in jail or in a hospital. But Marlowe survives because people underestimate him. Augustine, Lennox, and Eileen Wade (Nina van Pallandt) dismiss him as a dupe. Even after he tracks down Lennox, Terry refuses to accept Marlowe as a threat, telling him, "If you're thinking of making trouble for me, forget it . . . before you can convince anybody that the suicide was a fake, I'll be long gone." His smugness infuriates the detective, while the mention of the "suicide" gives Marlowe an idea and suggests his course of action. Having never learned the self-serving morality that Lennox asserts, Marlowe still determines right and wrong by his own implacable standards. Terry argues that Marlowe is "breaking the law" when he points a gun at him, but Marlowe responds, "Believe me, that's the last thing I'm breaking." Marlowe knows he cannot have Lennox arrested and charged with the murder of his wife, Sylvia. He figures that he can shoot Lennox with impunity. Deceit and betrayal are also important considerations for Marlowe. So he tells Lennox, "You lied to me, my neck was out to here. With the cops, with Marty Augustine, and all the way along the line I'm pulling for you." Here Altman is not interested in creating a mythic figure. Marlowe is just human. Outrage and revenge are in this case acceptable motivations for him.

The actual murder of Lennox is in keeping with the best traditions of the genre: *The Big Sleep*, for example, ends with Marlowe causing the death of a hoodlum who tried to betray him. The shockingly unique aspect of *The Long Goodbye* is Marlowe's cheerful attitude about the murder. He walks away from the corpse and begins playing a harmonica; he lightly skips down the road, ignoring Eileen Wade and forgetting what just occurred. Marlowe is satisfied with this act of revenge.

So just as *McCabe and Mrs. Miller* eroded the genre of the western, *The Long Goodbye* works consistently to end the heroic and mythic connotations of the private detective. Marlowe's attitude toward the murder is reinforced immediately by the soundtrack, which begins a "Hooray for Hollywood" cheer as Marlowe leaves the scene of the crime. Reference to films abound in *The Long Goodbye*, reminding the viewer of Marlowe's fictional nature, undermining the fantasy of Marlowe as the protector of freedom.

The Long Goodbye is another concrete example of Altman's awareness and use of cinematic traditions. Altman directly alludes to *The Thin Man* (when Marlowe mentions Asta) and *The Invisible Man* (with Marlowe's comments to the bandaged patient in his hospital room). The death of Roger Wade (Sterling Hayden) seems most like a reenactment of the suicide in *A Star Is Born*. The Mexican funeral procession appears borrowed from *Greed*. The Malibu security guard imitates Barbara Stanwyck in *Double Indemnity*. (Chandler wrote the screenplay for that film.) The guard's imitation of Cary Grant is not coincidence; Grant was Chandler's first choice for Marlowe. These allusions indicate the cinematic past from which the director draws. They also complement his indictment of the easy morality and insubstantial values of Hollywood.

Hesitant about the film's chances for success, United Artists opened *The Long Goodbye* in Los Angeles, without much advance publicity. At that time a Los Angeles premiere was a curious strategy, since nearly all major-studio films opened in New York City and Altman's films have historically had their best box-office draw there. One could not reasonably predict that a film so critical of the Hollywood/West Coast life-style would be welcomed in Los Angeles. Predictably, the film flopped, and distribution ceased shortly thereafter. Six months later United Artists began a new campaign for *The Long Goodbye*, stressing it as a comic approach to murder-mystery. When it opened in large cities through the country, however, the film still did not attract many viewers.

During the release and the hiatus preceding the redistribution, *The Long Goodbye* met with a divided critical reception. Charles Gregory, in *Sight and Sound* and *Film Quarterly*, attacked the depiction of Marlowe, stating that "one cannot satirize or destroy a hero image until one defines it . . . thus Philip Marlowe is not only a nebbish, but a victim in the hands of Robert Altman."[2] Pauline Kael, in her review "Movieland—The Bums' Paradise," commented that "the negative reviews kept insisting that Altman's movie had nothing to do with Chandler's novel and that Elliot Gould wasn't Marlowe. People still want to believe that Galahad is alive and well and living in Los Angeles."[3] Later reviews, particularly those of Robert Hatch in the *Nation*, Philip French in *Sight and Sound*, Garrett Stewart in *Film Quarterly*, and Colin L. Westerbeck in *Commonweal*, praised the film highly. Even *Sight and Sound* (spring issue, 1975) reversed its original evaluation of *The Long Goodbye* and included two favorable analyses of camera movement and the use of the musical soundtrack in the film. In time, *The Long Goodbye* was more widely accepted. It was regarded by one critic as the Altman "masterwork."

Thieves Like Us

While *The Long Goodbye* was being completed, producer Jerry Bick, through United Artists, acquired the rights to the Edward Anderson novel *Thieves Like Us*, which was originally filmed in 1948 by Nicholas Ray as *They Live by Night*. In Anderson's novel, set in the 1930s, three convicts named Bowie, T-Dub, and Chicamaw escape from prison and reunite on occasions to rob banks in the South. T-Dub marries his girlfriend Lula, just before he is shot attempting to rob a bank with Chicamaw. Chicamaw is recaptured. Bowie, who has been living with his girlfriend Keechie, rescues Chicamaw from prison but abandons him on a country road. Bowie and Keechie are then killed in a police ambush.

Anderson's extended characterization of Bowie naturally appealed to Altman. (Bowie shares many of the same tragic delusions about life and freedom as Brewster McCloud and John McCabe.) Altman rejected a treatment written by Calder Willingham for Jerry Bick because it concentrated too heavily on the mechanics of the robberies and the chase scenes and hired Joan Tewkesbury, who had been a continuity assistant on *McCabe and Mrs. Miller,* to write an adaptation.

Tewkesbury welcomed the assignment. She enjoyed working again with the actors from *McCabe* who were cast for the film. She thought it "was like inviting old friends into your living room, taking off your shoes, and listening to them every time you wrote a line. I just wrote to their sensibility." She also had good rapport with Altman, and she liked the source material itself. She said about the director that he "so trusts his own instincts that you trust yours just because you think you should." Finally, she thought the Anderson novel was "one of the most beautiful books I've ever read." She felt all she had to do was "just pick the best stuff and glue it all together," and her 122-page screenplay did largely remain faithful to the novel. She tried to set the theme of the film within the characterizations, so that the settings and the plot could change while the theme remained consistent. In fact she recalled that "when we did *Thieves Like Us* whole sites would change, or the whole way we should dress a scene would change."[4]

So Tewkesbury did much more than simply "glue the pieces together" in her screenplay; she outlined specific thematic development and foreshadowings suggested by the book. In her script the concept of "thieves" did not only apply to bank robbers. As T-Dub states, the bankers, politicians, and doctors are the thieves and swindlers. Bowie, too, understands that "them capitalist fellows are thieves like us." In fact, Tewkesbury gives Bowie a strong code of ethics ("I never robbed nobody that couldn't stand to lose it"), which Anderson only implies.

The screenplay carefully foreshadows the fated lives of the convicts. For example, T-Dub believes that "laws [policemen] would be uptight if it wasn't for sore women and snitches" just before these two types cause his death. T-Dub senses that "when they get me again I won't be in any shape for a lawyer or anything else in this world." The shooting at the hotel proves that prediction. Bowie's life is ruled by superstition: he even interprets the numbers of license plates as ill omens. His fears are confirmed when he is killed near cabin 13 at Mattie's Grapes Motor Home. Chicamaw stresses to Bowie that the worst part of prison life for him was that the guards called him "old thing." When he is recaptured the prison captain refers once again to Chicamaw as "old thing," and for that remark the captain dies.

The most significant change from novel to screenplay was the survival of Bowie's girlfriend Keechie. When asked why Keechie did not die at the

Keith Carradine as Bowie helps John Schuck as Chicamaw escape in Thieves. *Courtesy of United Artists, New York, NY.*

end, as Anderson had intended, Tewkesbury explained that "it was the producer's feeling that if Keechie also died at the end, it would be just like *Bonnie and Clyde.*"

Altman also subjected the screenplay to another "streamlining" in the shooting, the same as he did in *McCabe and Mrs. Miller* and *The Long Goodbye.* The film does not explain how the convicts organized their escape, although the operation is described in detail in the source works. The film does not show, for example, how Bowie acquires the sheriff's uniform and credentials used for Chicamaw's escape from prison—a maneuver of Bowie's that is stressed in the writing. Finally, the film deletes the character of Judge Hawkins, who assists Bowie and Keechie in both the novel and screenplay. It seems therefore that in many ways the loose narrative structure was accomplished in the shooting and editing of the film, and not in the writing of the screenplay.

Altman also used radio programs and news flashes in the background soundtrack to comment ironically on the convicts' marginally successful robberies and their love affairs. The pacing, the settings, and the mannerisms of the convicts in *Thieves* pointedly differ from Nicholas Ray's version of *Thieves* (see Robert Kolker's "Night to Day" article in *Sight and Sound*, Autumn 1974).

Altman faced many serious obstacles during the forty-three days of location shooting. One of the major problems was the weather. Tewkesbury remarked that "we got more rain than you can imagine and got flooded out of numerous locations." Rain delays were especially serious since Altman's $1.25 million budget would not permit extensive set construction or adjustments. He was forced to find the locations he desired in the rural South and to use those towns and setting as they stood.

Altman was also without the services of his usual cinematographer and art director. Mark Rydell (who had agreed to play Marty Augustine in *The Long Goodbye* in order to watch Altman work) had hired Vilmos Zsigmond and Leon Erickson for his new film *Cinderella Liberty*. Altman employed cinematographer Jean Boffety, who had never worked in the United States, and assigned his friend Scottie Bushnell as a visual consultant, to compensate for his missing art director. Bushnell served as associate producer and casting consultant on most of Altman's following films.

The director hired Jerry Bick's wife, Louise Fletcher, to play the role of Mattie. Altman intended Mattie to be a minor character in the film, but he was so impressed by Fletcher's performance that he expanded the role. Mattie became the gang's cook and domestic coordinator, surrogate mother and savior of Keechie, and the betrayer of Bowie.

Two of the leads in this film, Bert Remsen and John Schuck, had previously been given minor parts in several Altman films. The roles of T-Dub, the lame "mastermind" of the gang, and Chicamaw, the psychotic who robs bankers for the sake of publicity, were quite complex. The roles were great opportunities for the men, and their performances were superb. Schuck nonetheless abandoned his film career for various television spots ("McMillan and Wife") after *Thieves*, while Remsen appeared in comic roles in a succession of Altman films.

The main proponent of the talents of Keith Carradine and Shelley Duvall as Bowie and Keechie in *Thieves Like Us* was Pauline Kael. In her "Love and Coca-Cola" article she described how "Keith Carradine takes the screen the way a star does, by talent and by natural right," while Shelley Duvall "carries candor to the point of eccentricity: she's so natural that she seems bizarrely original . . . her charm appears to be totally without affectation." For Kael *Thieves* was "the closest to flawless of Altman's films."[5]

Thieves Like Us received similarly favorable reviews from critics across the country. Many agreed that Altman had, for the first time, captured the mood and sentiments of Faulkner on film. Some critics recognized that, despite its similarites to *Bonnie and Clyde*, *Thieves Like Us* did not exploit violence or praise the criminals as did Arthur Penn's film.[6]

The biggest flaw in *Thieves* is Altman's repeated use of radio shows as voice-over narrations. When Bowie and Keechie begin to express physical intimacies, the radio announcer for the "Shakespeare on the Air" show is saying, "Thus did Romeo and Juliet consummate their first encounter by falling in love with each other." As their naive love-making continues, that same announcement is repeated three times. Instead of achieving an intended comic effect Altman only succeeds in exasperating the patience of the viewer.

The film's humor is best when it is organic and underplayed. The door to Bowie's room falls from its hinges when Dee Mobley (Tom Skerritt) exits. By shooting the scene from a distance, the director achieved a relaxed and subtle comic effect not evident in the use of the radio shows.

Despite critical approval, the public did not respond favorably to *Thieves Like Us*. The film opened in New York and Washington and closed in both cities within a few weeks. United Artists had so little faith in the success of the film it never bothered with publicity; the studio accepted the loss and quickly withdrew the film from distribution.

California Split

Unaffected by the lack of popular support for *Thieves* and bolstered by the nearly unanimous positive critical sentiment, Altman began work in 1974 on a film called *California Split*, based on a sketchy Joseph Walsh screenplay about gambling in America. While the dominant characteristics of *Thieves Like Us* are inevitability and somber detachment, *California Split* flourishes with excitement, tension, emotional and psychological conflicts of great magnitude, cynicism, and slapstick humor.

The film relates the story of two inveterate gamblers, Charlie Waters (Elliott Gould) and Bill Denny (George Segal), who meet at a card table in a Los Angeles poker parlor. They share a passion for all types of gambling but have quite different personalities. Charlie lives spontaneously, enjoying himself whether winning or losing. Bill is more conservative. Tied to a job with a magazine and recently separated from his wife, he views gambling as a risky means of escape. For Charlie it is an entire life-style. Charlie and Bill have one kind of luck—bad. They lose at poker and at dog races. When they win at the race-track and at a boxing match they are robbed. The men decide to pool their resources and go to Reno, Nevada, to make a "killing" in the casinos. Bill begins his winning streak in a high-stakes poker game. He continues to amass over eighty thousand dollars playing blackjack, roulette, and craps. Charlie is elated, but for Bill the special feeling he had for gambling disappears. Charlie tries to cheer him, wondering if he "always take[s] a win this hard." Bill remains disoriented, unable to enjoy the money, wondering if there is really any meaning to this big win. Less philosophically, Charlie splits their winnings and leaves the casino to "live it up" and keep on gambling.

Altman and cinematographer Paul Lohmann (whom Altman retained to photograph most of his films after *California Split*) wanted to make the film appear as realistic as possible. They shot the poker parlor scenes, for example, with available light. The fluorescent bulbs gave the print a green tint that Altman retained to a degree to capture the artificiality of the parlor. Altman recognized the importance of simultaneous action, overhead conversations, and distractions in casino gambling. He therefore employed multiple microphones inside the casino. To lend further authenticity to the casino segment, the director convinced professional cardplayers such as "Amarillo Slim" Preston to take part in Bill's cutthroat poker game. Reinforced by their own personal experiences with gambling, Altman and scenarist-coproducer-actor Walsh added details to the script—and these small touches contributed to the overwhelming sense of spontaneity.

The director called *California Split* a celebration of gambling. The excitement and humor are largely generated by Elliott Gould. His cynical musings at the Pasadena Poker parlor; his outrageous attempt to pacify Susan (Gwen Welles) with the story of the sperm whale; his insistence on identifying Dumbo and Snoopy as two of the seven dwarfs; his victory over the bully Lew (Edward Walsh); and his desperation in the Reno casino—playing nickel slot machines and wagering candy bars at blackjack—define Gould as the center of attraction, as the affable hero. Segal never attempts to "top" Gould. He avoids playing Hawkeye to Gould's Trapper John.

Bill enjoys himself while in Charlie's company, and he trusts him, but nonetheless he maintains his individuality. The two men do not, as some critics suggest, represent one manic-depressive personality. Gould and Segal do not allow the kinship of Charlie and Bill to deteriorate into the Newman/Redford realm of facile acceptance and superficial ties. They are witty and attractive characters, but they are independent men with separate goals and life-styles.

The theme of *California Split* may be deduced from its title. The term "California split," which is slang for big-stakes, high/low poker games, also refers to Charlie and Bill's conflicting motivations for gambling: the overriding desire to "win big" versus the sheer excitement of living on the edge between instant wealth and financial ruin. Winning or losing makes little difference to Charlie. His important concern is living with "the action." Bill deludes himself into thinking that he is like Charlie, but after his run of luck he realizes that gambling holds no similar fascination for him. Charlie is ready, after leaving Reno, to "live for a year," gambling at every occasion, but Bill is disenchanted. The win provides Charlie with the capital to retreat further into the fantasies upon which he has structured his life. Charlie guesses that, for Bill, "it doesn't mean a fucking thing, does it?" Once Bill recognizes that he could never repeat his actions, he chooses to return to the "home" he had previously abandoned, perhaps forsaking the role of the compulsive gambler. Gambling means freedom for Charlie; for the high-strung Bill it is a sporadic addiction.

Critical reception of *California Split* was typically divided between Altman supporters, who judged the film to be "perhaps the best film ever made about gambling," and his detractors, who thought the film "monomaniacal." Few critics seemed to recognize that the film was brilliant and flawed; that its characters were wonderfully authentic and enjoyable, but that it was difficult to isolate exactly what the phenomenon of gambling, as portrayed in the film, implied about American culture.

Altman was clearly in love with his subject. Although he did not make the film for its commercial appeal, *California Split* had the best chance of any of his previous films since *M*A*S*H* of reaching a wide and diverse audience. It dealt with a popular topic in comic style. It starred two of Hollywood's most prominent actors. Upon its release in the summer of 1974, it grossed only $5 million. There seemed to be minimal interest in a thought-provoking or controversial film about gambling. Columbia Pictures immediately ceased distribution; *California Split* was sold to ABC for a television showing within two years.

The fact that the film did not return a more sizable profit was not discouraging to Altman. In fact, he has good reason to be proud of this film. The episodes he selects to portray the ups and downs of the lives of Charlie and Bill are quite imaginative and appropriate. The characters' relationships with women in the film are complex, and Altman seems to catch enough of the glances and nuances of conversation exchanged among the characters to make the viewer feel that these interactions could occur exactly as they are shown. Also the byplay and betting between Charlie and Bill about Dumbo and basketball are hilarious. Altman suggests in *California Split* that between the cards or before the throw of the dice the gambler experiences a fear, a fever, an exhilaration, a panic more intense than any other experience in life, and win or lose, that moment is an existential trauma. The experience leaves Charlie wanting more, and Bill feeling depressed. Bill recognizes that the elation is transient, and Charlie will never stop chasing it. The traps that gambling holds for them are amusing and frightening, and completely realistic.

During the making of *California Split* Robert Altman had been watching the progress of Joan Tewkesbury. She was working for him on a script dealing with the popularity of country music that would prove to be his masterpiece.

7

Nashville

NASHVILLE IS THE HIGHPOINT of Robert Altman's film career. Clearly his most controversial film, *Nashville* was also his most successful gamble. He developed innovative production techniques to relate a story based on twenty-four major characters. With its explosive political content, *Nashville* altered the tradition of the conservative film musical, demanding much of its viewers and offering no easy interpretations.

Consistent with Altman's later films, *Nashville* examined the widespread presence of apathy and complacency in American culture. The tone of *Nashville*, however, is not hostility, but objectivity. *Nashville* does not advocate an explicit ideological perspective, but it does suggest the need for a moral reawakening of the United States.

Story Line

The city of Nashville, called the Athens of the South, is commencing its Grand Ole Opry celebration. The festivities center on the arrival of Barbara Jean (Ronee Blakley), the "first lady" of country music, at a Nashville airport. Inside the terminal, throngs of fans mix with singing stars and with the campaign workers of a radical new political party. Before Barbara Jean can greet her followers, she faints and is carried to an ambulance. Her devotees quickly leave the terminal.

Throughout ensuing traffic jams and collisions Altman introduces other major characters: country-western singer Haven Hamilton (Henry Gibson), his mistress Lady Pearl (Barbara Baxley), and his son Buddy (David Peel); Hamilton's lawyer Delbert Reese (Ned Beatty); popular black singer Tommy Brown (Timothy Brown); Opal, a BBC reporter (Geraldine Chaplin); Kenny Fraiser (David Hayward), a young visitor to Nashville; and Albuquerque (Barbara Harris), an "undiscovered" singer who has run away from Star (Bert Remsen), her husband.

In successive scenes, the director explicates the shallow and parasitic nature of character interactions. The Reeses' marriage, for example, lacks real communication. Their children are deaf, and Delbert does not under-

73

Barbara Harris as Albuquerque saves the day at the Parthenon
in Nashville. *Courtesy of Paramount Pictures Press Release,*
Los Angeles, CA.

stand sign language. John Triplette (Michael Murphy), the public-relations man for the Hal Philip Walker presidential campaign, uses Delbert to arrange interviews with Haven Hamilton and Barbara Jean. Haven's alliance with Barbara Jean helps keep him in the spotlight while she recovers from nervous exhaustion. Barbara Jean's husband, Barnett (Allen Garfield), is sadistic and self-serving in his emotional badgering of his wife.

The film then follows the progress of Triplette's infiltration of the country-western music scene, documenting the growth in his prestige in the upper echelons of the music industry. He offers Hamilton the governorship of Tennessee for supporting Walker. He forces Barnett to underwrite Barbara Jean's appearance at an outdoor rally at the Parthenon after she suffers another nervous collapse at the Opry Belle.

Triplette and Delbert Reese cause the public humiliation of Sueleen Gay (Gwen Welles) at a Walker fundraising party. Meanwhile Linnea Reese (Lily Tomlin), ignored by her husband, joins the ranks of four other females having affairs with the folk singer Tom (Keith Carradine).

In-fighting between Barbara Jean and Connie White reaches its apex on a night of the Grand Ole Opry performance. Barbara Jean listens to the concert on the radio in her hospital room, gazing at a bouquet of black flowers sent to her by Connie's manager. Barnett presents Connie with one orchid wrapped in cellophane paper. Onstage at the Grand Ole Opry, Haven slights Connie by calling her "a wonderful singer in her own way," so she retaliates by insulting him, Barnett, and their guest, Julie Christie.

The next day, singers and their fans assemble for the outdoor pageant organized by Triplette. The event illustrates the compromises characters have made throughout the film. Fearing that a direct connection with the Walker party would alienate fans, Haven Hamiliton and Barbara Jean eventually decide that the benefits of media exposure are worth that risk. Unconcerned with their musical talents, Triplette gambles that their presence will draw a large crowd for his candidate in spite of the "ground rules" Barnett has requested. The fans are willing to tolerate political propaganda for the opportunity to see Nashville stars live.

One of the fans, however, has an ulterior motive for his presence. Having run away from home to escape a domineering mother, Kenny comes to Nashville to kill Barbara Jean. Dressed in white and singing about her "Idaho home," Barbara Jean has become an objectification of his hatred. He shoots her, instead of killing Hal Philip Walker, whom the viewer expects to be the target of an assassination attempt. Wounded by one of the pistol shots, Haven tries to calm the crowd, but now the fans feel shocked and betrayed. Staring at the Walker banner "New Roots for the Nation," the crowd joins with Albuquerque in an elegy on the loss of their Barbara Jean. While they sing "It Don't Worry Me," John Triplette, sensing that their excitement has turned into disenchantment, walks offstage, alone and defeated. The film closes with a slow camera tilt from the American flag to the sky, with Albuquerque's song in voice-over. This ambiguous ending suggests the sadness and frustration felt by those who witness the assassination. It also highlights the resilience and optimism that they share.

Production

Nashville was filmed on location in the summer of 1974 on a $3 million budget. The film was shot in sequence, so for those seven weeks the entire cast and crew camped at a Nashville motel. The film was in every way a risky, communal undertaking, with the director acting as a combined authority figure/summer-camp counselor. He took the cast on a bus "to every location we picked, so they had a physical feeling of what the space was."[1] Improvisations of dialogue occurred during rehearsals. Individual and group discussions of scenes and script continued throughout the filming. Daily rushes were viewed by all members of the *Nashville* family.

Cast members and Altman negotiated agreements about the personalities of the characters in the film. Michael Murphy revealed, for example, that the result of his collaborative efforts with Altman on the characterization of John Triplette was "a few moments that really make him [Triplette] look more human."[2] Confident in the judgment and abilities of his performers, Altman encouraged them to lend their own personal backgrounds to the characters, to contribute or vary dialogue, and especially to write the lyrics for their songs. The injuries that Ronee Blakley had actually sustained in a fire were incorporated into the Barbara Jean background as a "tragic incident with a fire baton." Blakley wrote five songs for the film and invented the monologue for her onstage breakdown.

Both newcomers and Altman veterans appreciated this opportunity to experiment with artistic expression. Blakley stated, "There was no fear in me, the novice, for the famous director." Henry Gibson, who had formerly appeared as Dr. Verringer, the psychiatrist in *The Long Goodbye*, felt that "there was no star system, no rank-pulling" in the production of *Nashville*.[3] Cast members expressed faith in Altman's decisions, with the exception of Allen Garfield, whose violent arguments with Altman reached near-fisticuffs during the final days of shooting. The Barnett-Triplette encounter on the Parthenon stage alludes to the volatile Altman-Garfield relationship.

Altman explained that this "considerable amount of freedom" was integral to his working methods for *Nashville*, since "what we do is set up the arena and create an event. Then we cover it as though it were actually happening." This unique process of invention was reflected in the shooting style, in the use of sound, and in the development of the script.

Sid Levin, one of *Nashville*'s editors, clarified the difference between Altman's approach to his subject and a "classical" shooting style. Altman did not break down each scene into long, medium, and close-up shots, but instead used a greater number of master angles to give actors greater flexibility. Altman also worked without shooting sketches for many background settings and crowds, and so assistant directors Tommy Thompson and Alan Rudolph often created "their own movie" in the background. With over 300,000 feet of film—two times the usual amount of film shot for a Hollywood project of the same running time—Altman felt free to play with the different possibilities created by this approach.[4]

The innovative technical use of eight-track and Chemtone processes complemented the unorthodox shooting style of *Nashville*. Lion's Gate Eight-Track Sound System was refined from a concept that Jim Webb and Chris McLaughlin originated during the filming of *California Split*. The system recorded or "mixed" multiple-sourced live sound from separate microphones within and outside the frame. Since the sound was transmitted on microwave, Altman no longer needed mike booms and umbilical microphones. The camera could therefore be placed virtually anywhere he desired, permitting a wider shot selection, more camera movement, and varying angles of approach.

The sound system also eliminated the need for postdubbing, which typically deadens any sound effect. Since all sound was recorded separately and synchronously during the shooting, it was unnecessary to add sounds to match the action during the editing stages. The authenticity, clarity, and immediacy of sound recording in *Nashville* remain unparalleled.

The complexity of sound enriched the smooth development of the narrative in *Nashville*. Overlapping dialogue, sound effects, and background commentary effectively utilized all sound tracks, so sixteen additional tracks were added for recording the songs and background music. This addition provided still greater freedom for Altman since there was always enough background "noise" to establish a sensible transition between visually disparate scenes.

Chemtone processing, developed by the TCV labs, gave Altman a great deal of flexibility in lighting *Nashville*. The processing increases a filmstock's sensitivity to color. More sophisticated than the "flashing" used by Altman in *The Long Goodbye*, it permitted him to shoot under unfavorable lighting conditions and to adjust shades and color saturation later. This process, along with a refinement of Lion's Gate Eight-Track Sound, freed him from traditional cinematic restraints and permitted him to create an impressionistic and spontaneous feeling in the film.

The evolution of the *Nashville* script illustrates Altman's confidence in creative collaboration and his effectiveness with the "arena" approach. After rejecting a script called "The Great Southern Amusement Company," which superficially treated the topic of country music, Altman in 1972 hired Joan Tewkesbury, his co-writer on *Thieves Like Us*, to devise an original screenplay on that topic. The only condition that Altman stipulated was that someone should die at the end. Tewkesbury then visited Nashville several times and drew the events of the film from her own observations of the Nashville music scene. She described the full-length screenplay as "never hard-edged . . . situations that were left open for, first, Altman to fill out, and then for the actor to fill out." Her screenplay was submitted without a political subtext.

In 1973 she and Altman began adding characters and dialogue. The Hal Philip Walker campaign, for example, was added with the break of Watergate. By January 1974 the actors were given a 176-page screenplay. That spring Alan Rudolph, Altman's assistant director for *The Long Goodbye*, *California Split*, and *Nashville*, wrote the shooting script for the film. Tewkesbury stated that Rudolph "stripped down all the descriptions and left in the dialogue and just gave real short actions."[5] Altman reiterated Tewkesbury's description of the "final step"—the creative involvement of the actors. He explained that "most of the improvisation came in terms of rehearsal, and then things were set." The 1974 Altman-Tewkesbury revision fulfilled a vital organizational function for the director. He believed that the dialogue was an important framework for the scenes, but that it did not have to be used, and that "as long as it can be improved, and made more honest, then we will do that." Some actors, such as Keenan Wynn, who played Mr. Green, gave their lines exactly as written. Other cast members added their own experience, mannerisms, and speech idioms to their characters. Gwen Welles, for example, had rehearsed her role by working at a Nashville airport lunch counter, and thus could expertly portray the optimism, humor, and pathos of Sueleen Gay.

Reception

The postproduction editing of *Nashville* sparked one of the hottest controversies in the history of popular film criticism. Various critics, including Pauline Kael, Judith Crist, Bruce Williamson, Charles Michener, and Hollis Alpert, viewed the footage as it was cut from the daily rushes and trimmed to eight hours, six hours, three and a half, and under three hours in length. Of these critics, Kael and Alpert, who had "dropped by for a drink one night," probably saw the most footage and viewed a "two-thirds cut" of approximately six hours in length. According to Alpert, "Just seeing the rushes was, for me, exciting." He could therefore understand why Pauline Kael had then breached "what is considered rightful and normal critical practice"[6] when on 26 February 1975, she ecstatically reviewed the most recent three-hour rough cut of *Nashville* for the *New Yorker*. She took the opportunity to argue against conglomerate control of the film industry and urged Paramount to release a longer version of the film.[7]

Since *Nashville* was due for release during Kael's half-year absence from the *New Yorker*, the review was personally expedient for Kael and for Altman. The ethical debate on the issue of reviewing a film before its final cut created more publicity for *Nashville*. The rough cut of *Nashville* viewed by Kael and others was shortened by approximately fifteen minutes to a running time of 159 minutes. The film remained largely the same. Altman eliminated some of the sixty songs he had recorded live for the film; he also removed some less significant scenes. For example, in the longer version, Opal states that she was not at the moment working for the BBC, but was doing an article for *Cahiers du Cinéma*. On another occasion Triplette reveals that his wife left him for an actor.

Andrew Sarris overstated his case when complaining that Kael's early, favorable review was unwarranted, but Pauline Kael seemed unduly influenced by outtakes from the film when arguing for a longer version of *Nashville*. Like Kael, John Simon was upset by what he feared had been deleted. He concluded that Paramount had done Altman "a grave disservice."[8] He ignored the fact that the final decision of running length resided solely with Altman, not with Paramount, or with the executive producers for ABC, Jerry Weintraub and Martin Starger. When asked if he was subjected to any pressure to cut *Nashville* to some maximum length, Altman responded that "there were a lot of people biting their tongues. They were nervous that the film came out as long as it did." His entire television and film career demonstrates his insistence on artistic control. Altman would tolerate no studio intrusion in determining the length of *Nashville*, a film he once described as "my Grand Hotel," so it was released exactly as he desired.

The film was fairly well received upon its release in the summer of 1975. Despite problems with projection and sound, Nashville drew sizable crowds. The film grossed $10 million within a year after its release—far below the expectations of Paramount, but enough to turn a small profit for Altman. Critical response to the film was very favorable. Highest praise, besides Kael's, came from Hollis Alpert, Tom Wicker, Charles Michener in a *Newsweek* cover story, Chris Hodenfield for *Rolling Stone*, and Connie Byrne and William Lopez in *Film Quarterly*. The New York Film Critics gave *Nashville* awards for Best Film, Best Director, and Best Supporting Actress (Lily Tomlin), and "I'm Easy" won an Academy Award for Best Song.

Other critics admired the film but had some serious reservations. Roger Greenspun felt that the film was "marvelous in its incidentals and only bad in its most gratuitous element—the main plot." John Simon objected to its "uneasy symbolism." Stanley Kauffmann criticized "some banalities of image" and a "consciously fey style" and Jay Cocks praised only Lily Tomlin's performance.

Other critics were more scathing in their attacks on the film. Manny Farber and Paul Krassner launched virtual vendettas against *Nashville* on social and political grounds. Joel Siegel in *Film Heritage* condemned "Gnashville" for its shallowness, while John Malone argued in the *New York Times* that the film's treatment of women constituted "celluloid rape." In general, the same critics (except for Simon and Kauffmann) who liked previous Altman films also praised *Nashville*. A strong movement against *Nashville* came from those critics who had attacked Altman's other films.

Symbolism

Symbolism and plot are the most common problem in analyses of *Nashville*. Symbolism in the film appears heavy-handed, and characters often seem to drift randomly from one event to the next within the five-day period, without logic, motivation, and background. On the other hand, much of the film's appeal lies in its openness: there are no hidden messages, disguised references, or arcane allusions. Characters are revealed as interesting, complex, or puzzling through the course of their normal interactions with one another. Their archetypal significance is therefore minimal. When signs and symbols are used in *Nashville*, they do not flow easily from the narrative, nor do they contribute much to the development of theme.

Conventional symbolism is employed sparingly in *Nashville*, and in rather unsophisticated ways. Barbara Jean's and Haven Hamilton's white clothes establish them as innocent and unsuspecting victims marked for slaying. Kenny Fraiser's violin case seems borrowed from ganster films of the 1930s and 1940s. Tom's tape recorder, which constantly plays his voice, portrays his insecurity and his fear of being alone. The motorcyclist/magician may represent an inexplicable phenomenon shared by all the characters (i.e., the death of Barbara Jean). His sleight-of-hand tricks convey the facile deceptions practiced by the Hal Philip Walker campaign workers. In each case, symbolism is blatant. Altman refrained from burdening the film with too many intricate references, but the few symbolic objects, characters, and events he chose to incorporate into the film appear obvious and contrived.

Nashville is carefully structured around specific characterizations. The film is not a compilation of vignettes lacking an overall plan; but throughout the film, plot is subordinate to character development. There are two distinct narrative modes affecting character interactions in the film. First, all characters encounter and respond to the political and personal manipulations of John Triplette. The Walker public-relations man influences the lives of each of the twenty-three other characters, and eventually they all accede to his wishes. Altman adds a second layer of structure to the film by grouping the characters into smaller sets of discrete alliances. *Nashville* shows us familial, sexual, and professional relationship in various stages of dissolution, depicting the characters' pathetic movement from initial liaisons to inevitable rejections and estrangements.

In her book summarizing plots and themes in Altman films, Judith Kass implies that Opal and Triplette function as alternating narrators in *Nashville*, with Triplette representing the characters' political views and Opal uniting those people involved in the music industry. But a Triplette/Opal dichotomy is an interpretation antithetical to the dominant thematic movement in *Nashville* of blurring of distinctions between politics and business. Also, Opal cannot serve as a locus of character unity because she does not meet all the music-industry characters, nor does she interact with them at crucial moments in the film. She is continually excluded from professional gatherings by Haven Hamilton. She is absent during Barbara Jean's breakdowns at the airport and at the Opry Belle. She also misses the shooting of Barbara Jean at the Parthenon.

John Triplette is a glib, charismatic, Madison Avenue con artist, hired by the Replacement party to act as their advance man, preparing media coverage and local support for Walker's personal appearance in Nashville. He meets all the characters in the film except for Kenny, Private Kelly (Scott Glenn), and Wade (Robert Doqui). He is on camera more than any other character in the film. He makes whatever promises are necessary to ingratiate his candidate with the music industry rank and file. He guarantees Haven Hamilton the support of the Walker organization if Hamilton should decide to run for the governorship of Tennessee. Triplette persuades the folksinger Bill (Allan Nicholls) to support Walker, assuring Bill's group of a "big audience from these country guys," from "local yokels" like Haven Hamilton. Ironically, Triplette personifies Walker's disclaimful description of lawyers who are trained to clarify and to confuse, "whichever is to his client's advantage." He denies or lies about his intentions to everyone in Nashville. In his sales pitch he is either "the last guy in the world to try and change your mind about something you don't want to do," or he is "certainly not here to sell you a bill of goods." With the exception of one argument with Barnett, Triplette maintains that low-key, no-pressure image. Content with controlling the flow of events from behind the scenes,

Henry Gibson as Haven Hamilton in two crucial moments in Nashville. *Courtesy of Paramount Pictures Press Release, Los Angeles, CA.*

he awaits opportune moments to make his move. Then with tactics ranging from extortion to emotional blackmail, he plays upon the greed and
rivalries of the leading country-western stars.

The narrative of *Nashville* documents Triplette's methodical attempts to
capitalize on the popularity and gullibility of Nashville stars in order to
widen Walker's appeal in the South. He is successively drawn into the
complexities and contradictions of the music industry. He develops four
significant links to the music scene. Reese introduces him to Haven Hamilton, Barnett, Sueleen Gay, and Bill, each of whom provides avenues for
Triplette's assault on the industry.

Haven Hamilton's explanation of the Connie White–Barbara Jean rival-
ry sets up the film's dominant contrast between Connie White's calculated
artifice and Barbara Jean's natural charm. With Haven's assistance, Triplette learns that, although Hamilton and White may each have loyal fans,
Barbara Jean currently has the widest base of appeal. Then, in order to
win Barbara Jean's support, Triplette faces her husband, Barnett. When
Barbara Jean stops singing and begins her rambling soliloquy at the Opry
Belle, Barnett is "trapped." He does not wish to "cause a breach between
the fans and his fragile wife." The situation provides Triplette with the
perfect opportunity to convince Barnett to have Barbara Jean appear with
Haven Hamilton at the Parthenon. Kenny Fraiser and Private Kelly witness the breakdown and hear Barnett agree to the Parthenon performance. Their presence and their actions at the rally thus result from
Triplette's maneuvering of Barnett, from Kenny's own desire to kill the
singer, and from Kelly's expressed desire to be Barbara Jean's guardian.

Triplette's deals with Bill and with Sueleen Gay integrate the remaining
peripheral characters of *Nashville* with the mainstream of the narrative.
Bill, Mary (Christina Raines), Tom, Linnea, and Norman (David Arkin)
remain fairly isolated from the country-western and Walker scenes until
Triplette thrusts them into the political arena. When Triplette telephones
the Demon's Den bar in search of a "provocative" female entertainer for
his fund-raising party, Sueleen Gay becomes his prime candidate. Albuquerque is also at Demon's Den when Sueleen is propositioned. She
watches from backstage while Sueleen performs for the Walker group.
She overhears Triplette's promise to allow Sueleen to sing with Barbara
Jean at the Parthenon, if she finishes the act in a manner more in keeping
with the expectations of the drunken male crowd. Sueleen and Albuquerque, desperate to become stars, next surface on stage at the Walker rally,
with Wade and Star in hot pursuit. Their presence is another explicit man-
ifestation of Triplette's manipulations of people's lives to correspond with
his needs. His agreements with Bill and Sueleen also serve to unify the
characters whose connection with the central action of *Nashville* was tentative. The gathering of all characters in this film, ranging in importance

from Barbara Jean to L.A. Joan (Shelley Duvall), at the end of the film is therefore not coincidental.

Narrative structure in *Nashville* is also preserved within smaller groupings of characters. The *Nashville* population is classified within different sets of crumbling familial relationships, transient sexual alliances, broken friendships, or competing professional alliances.

Characters are joined through unstable and parasitic family ties. Each of the five families in *Nashville* evidences severe internal and external pressures. Haven Hamilton lives with his mistress, Lady Pearl, and his son Buddy, whose mother is in Europe. Secretly Buddy would rather be a singer than a lawyer for his father's corporation, but he is aware that his father would not permit that option. Meanwhile Haven must hide Lady Pearl from the public's eye. His performance of "For the Sake of the Children We Must Say Goodbye" at the Grand Ole Opry flaunts his hypocrisy and insensitivity. Further, Haven has an exploitative relationship with Buddy and Lady Pearl, who act as Haven's business managers and scapegoats.

The other families face similar, irresolvable problems. Delbert Reese is a professional yes-man who has neither the time nor the intelligence to establish more than superficial ties with his deaf children and gospel-singing, unfaithful wife. Mr. Green is mystified by his visiting niece Martha, who has rejected family ties and has even changed her name to L.A. Joan. She avoids visiting the dying Mrs. Green in the hospital and does not attend her funeral. Throughout the film Barnett views his wife as a commodity.

Nearly all characters in *Nashville* seek or are involved in casual sexual alliances. After Sueleen Gay sings "I Never Get Enough" and strips for the crowd of Walker supporters, Delbert Reese confesses to her, "I'd like to kiss you every place, you know what I'm telling you?" L.A. Joan's male friends include Buddy, Tricycle Man (Jeff Goldblum), Tom, and Kenny. Norman solicits Opal's affections, and allusions are made to her affairs with Buddy and with Elliott Gould. Wade propositions Linnea while she waits for Tom. Albuquerque's infidelity to Star is suggested throughout the film.

The character at the center of this sexual menagerie is the singer Tom, who, in the course of the film, sleeps with Mary, L.A. Joan, Opal, and Linnea. Tom even arranges his next affair before his current partner leaves his bedroom. Altman eloquently summarizes Tom's conquests in a brief scene in *Nashville*. Tom sings "I'm Easy," dedicating the song "to someone kind of special who just might be here tonight." At this announcement the director cuts from Opal, blushing, certain that the song was meant for her, to Mary, sitting uneasily next to her husband, Bill, then to L.A. Joan, who, like Opal, is flattered. The camera, following Tom's gaze, pans to Linnea, in the back of the inn. Soon Mary realizes that Tom is not looking at her and turns her head to spot his intended recipient. Opal, sitting at the same table as Mary, notices her action and also looks around the room. The pan continues to L.A. Joan, the last of the three women to be struck by the same unhappy perception. Tom's eyes are fixed on Linnea, and the camera also centers on her, showing the woman moved to tears by the emotional lyrics.

The song is a slap in the face to the three younger women, who eventually realize that they mean nothing to Tom. The short scene accentuates their pain and frustration by ending their affairs without the accusations and flaring tempers one might expect in similar confrontations. Tom's affair is then quickly terminated by Linnea. With this surprising reversal, Tom joins the ranks of the other pathetic victims of the transitory and exploitative sexual practices common in *Nashville*.

Finally, the characters are grouped by the professional affiliations and friendships they share, all of which are in a constant state of siege in *Nashville*. The stereotypic country-western music scene is in actuality quite heterogeneous, riddled with hatred and in-fighting. Connie White finds occasions to insult Barnett and Barbara Jean; Haven stabs Connie White in the back whenever possible. Hamilton lightly reveals industry factions to Triplette: "Connie White and Barbara Jean never appear on the stage together . . . and as for Haven Hamilton, well, I'll appear wherever Barbara Jean appears." Triplette repays Hamilton for his kindness by mocking his physical size and his costume while Tommy Brown and Haven perform at the Grand Ole Opry. Tommy Brown is well liked and respected by Haven and Barbara Jean, but their numerous racial slurs make his social connection to the Haven Hamilton–Barbara Jean complex appear tentative.

The incident that best conveys the unstable state of business affiliations involves the folk-singing trio of Tom, Bill, and Mary. Tom shocks Bill and Mary at the Exit Inn when he announces to the audience, "I *used* to be part of a trio," discarding them with no explanation. Alliances in Nashville do not permit sentimentality or courtesy.

Political Implications

Characters and events in *Nashville*, then, are logically organized and defined by their relationship to John Triplette, and by transitory allegiances. The story of *Nashville* is therefore told by examining the nature and implications of those character interactions. The methods of characterization, centering on Triplette's domination of Nashville and on disintegrating social relationships, suggest two related thematic conceits for *Nashville*: that the present structure of business and politics in America is essentially manipulative and corrupt, and that the decay of traditional social institutions reflects a complacent America motivated by greed and lust.

Nashville combines its disparaging political commentary with a satiric examination of the chaotic country-western scene. Music promotion and campaign practices appear equally contemptible; political platforms and song lyrics become indistinguishable. The film argues that politics and the entertainment industry have become two sides of the same coin. The juxtaposition of the opening Replacement party speech, for example, with the song "200 Years" reveals identical sophisms. Walker states that "we can do something about it [politics]," and Hamilton repeats, "It's up to us." Both systems manipulate the media for their respective clients. The news team covering the arrival of Barbara Jean puts her in the same shot with a Walker campaign worker. Haven Hamilton's Grand Ole Opry performance functions as his political debut, even though he adamantly proclaims that he has no interest in politics. Opal intertwines assassination theories with her interviews of stars at Lady Pearl's Pickin' Parlor.

Hal Philip Walker uses corporate metaphors to classify his audience as "fellow taxpayers and stockholders in America." The most forthright announcement of the marriage of politics and business occurs at the Parthenon concert. According to Barnett's "ground rules" for the concert, the performance will "never in any way, shape or form" associate Barbara Jean with Hal Philip Walker. Much to Barnett's dismay, the huge Replacement party banner, with its "New Roots for the Nation" exhortation, belies the spirit of his agreement with Triplette.

Political manipulation of the *Nashville* constituency relies on the same laughable credos, tactics, and slogans held dear by the corrupt country-western industry. At Opryland, the traditional Grand Ole Opry concert is just an excuse to sell Goo-Goo Candy Bars and King Leo Pure Stick Candy. Stockcars at the raceway, embossed with the names of favorite singing stars, and the Hal Philip Walker campaign van, touting its candidate's name through the streets of Nashville, accomplish the same thing.

Hal Philip Walker desires to replace "lawyeristic redtaped . . . government" with the "'yes' and 'no' language of farmers and teachers and engineers and businessmen," but both conglomerates actually appeal to a grass-roots following with inane slogans and clichés. Connie White sings that a "rolling stone gathers no moss" and Hal Philip Walker deduces that "there's no such thing as a free lunch." According to Walker's twisted logic, "When you pay more for an automobile than it cost Columbus to make his first voyage to America, that's politics." For Connie White, when you assure a child at the Grand Ole Opry that "any one of you could grow up to be the president," that's entertainment. The calculated sales pitches of the Walker campaign and of the country-western industry typically appeal to the lowest common denominator—the gullible average citizen. The *Nashville* politicians and stars seem determined to prove that no one ever went broke underestimating the intelligence of the American public.

The complacent acceptance of violence is a striking index of the decadence of society in *Nashville*. A representative incident involves a multiple car crash on a Nashville expressway. The collision initiates a free-for-all atmosphere. Those caught in the bumper-to-bumper traffic quickly abandon their cars en masse and join the party. Their favorite activities include autograph seeking, ambulance chasing, and fistfighting. Speaking over the blaring horns and sirens, Opal captures the frustration prevalent in the crowd behavior, stating, "It's America . . . all those mangled bodies." She complains, "I wish my cameraman had been here." The violent spectacle is acceptable and makes for a good story. Her enthusiasm and glee over the fracas define her motives as callous and sadistic.

Later, when Barbara Jean is shot at the Parthenon rally, Haven shouts amidst the sirens and screaming of the crowd, "They can't do this to us here in Nashville!"

Haven's philosophy conveys Altman's argument that "we can accept the assassination of the politician but not of the girl. Because we *condone* political assassination in our culture. We say that's all right, we understand that." Haven's objection reveals *Nashville's* primary goal: to describe a morally revolting and abusive social, political, and economic climate in America, which, if unchecked, will lead to the country's self-destruction.

The Musical Film as Cultural Indictment

With its twenty-seven songs and thirteen on-stage performances, *Nashville* appears to contain only the bare essentials of film musical. The director does include back stage production routines, but he focuses on the role of the media in defining and promoting musical performers and politicians as "stars." Playing off the traditional values of movie musicals, *Nashville* stands as an explicit cultural indictment. The city of Nashville, at the height of its yearly celebration, is the site of political opportunism, personal and moral degradation, and an assassination, all under the auspices of routine country-western promotion. *Nashville's* excoriating vision of complacency in American life and its widescale attack on hypocrisy continually break through the film's freewheeling, high-spirited, song-and-dance facade.

Such actively hostile views of American life and society had never surfaced in the musical genre. In the past fifteen years, dissidence and criticism of society had infiltrated and reshaped other genres of American film, but throughout this reorientation the film musical held its ground, impervious to changing times. Bob Fosse's *Cabaret* was one recent vehicle of

criticism, but even *Cabaret's* charges and hostilities were safely seques-
tered in the general brutality of pre–World War II Nazi Germany, far removed from the life and usual experiences of the average American
citizen. Altman had previously surprised viewers with his reversal of the
stereotypes found in the western and private-eye film; in doing so, he an-
ticipated a trend in filmmaking that reflected an increased dissatisfaction
with genre conventions. Similarly, *Nashville* works contrary to stereotypic
audience expectations for a musical.

The film musical always functioned to revitalize an already beleaguered
culture. *Singin' in the Rain* came closest to examining hypocritical American attitudes. But in *Singin' in the Rain*, as in *A Star Is Born*, cynicism
and disillusionment reflected some personal failing in an individual, some
isolated flaw, such as an unhappy childhood or an unnatural jealousy. The
analysis of the film industry in *Singin' in the Rain* merely provides "comic
mileage" for Kelly and Donen. Their film still reaffirmed the Alger success
story in the "Gotta Dance–Broadway Melody" sequence. The slapstick
humor in Donald O'Connor's "Make 'Em Laugh" routine called for unity
in the face of various hardships.

Behind their glitter and their lavish productions, film musicals have essentially reinforced the patriotic ideals and success myths described by
Robert Warshow and others. America was seen as a land of opportunity,
where through courage, hard work, and inventiveness one could "reach
the top." Popular musicals such as *Footlight Parade*, *The Gold-Diggers of
1933*, and *Yankee Doodle Dandy* provided interchangeable scenarios of
that success theme. But more importantly, they always solidified the culture in its moment of crisis, offering the unshakable belief that "everything
will work out all right if we just stick together." The characters in musicals
were filled with a contagious enthusiasm. Song and dance were the spontaneous expressions of that free spirit and overwhelming positive energy.
Fred Astaire's compulsive behavior in Mark Sandrich's *Top Hat* and the
"America" production number from Robert Wise's *West Side Story* typify
themes of freedom and optimism that the best film musicals have shared.

The same words of optimism, dedication, and common sense that ear-
marked that genre are echoed in the songs of *Nashville*, but not in the
same spirit. The songs depict a divided and irresolute America. Henry
Gibson's "200 Years" and "Keep A-Goin'" prescribe quasi-religious patriotism and mule-headed stubbornness as cure-alls for the problems of day-
to-day life. The Keith Carradine songs "It Don't Worry Me" and "I'm
Easy," on the other hand, establish apathy and detachment as ideal perspectives for the general public. Ronee Blakley's emotional rendition of
"My Idaho Home" suggests that through nostalgia and her family she
found happiness. Other typical country-western sentiments are expressed
in Karen Black's "Memphis" and "Rolling Stone," where life in America is

characterized as loveless, bleak and "getting darker," and filled with unrelenting pain and depression.

Nashville's attack on existing political and economic institutions is often far more subtle than the ironic refrain "We must be doing something right to last 200 years" would tend to indicate. In what is perhaps the best-edited musical sequence in *Nashville*—Timothy Brown's performance of "Blue-bird" on the Grand Ole Opry stage—life is defined as "that long lonesome road" that ideally includes "no money," "no kin," "no time clock." There is a veneer of freedom implied in the lyrics, but the viewer understands that the racial politics of Nashville will never allow Tommy Brown to find "the rainbow in my dreams."

For the characters in *Nashville* "life might be a one-way street"; yet they do not resent that imposed social and personal sterility. In fact, the lyrics that are repeated throughout the ending of the film, "you might say that I ain't free, but it don't worry me," provide an appropriate rallying point for Albuquerque and the crowd when Haven asks them to "show 'em what we're made of." So inundated by platitudes and false promises, the characters seek refuge in complacent and apathetic social attitudes. The weak characters in *Nashville* capitulate to corrupt forces they cannot alter and base their surrender on terms that enhance their material surroundings.

Characters in musicals before *Nashville* were motivated by honest ambition. If they were con men like Chester Kent in *Footlight Parade*, they acted for the good of "the show." In *Nashville* the a priori concerns are power and self-aggrandizement. Whether counted as fans or votes, the population of the city consists of easy marks for shrewd singing stars and manipulative politicans. Characters readily prostitute themselves to whatever extent necessary for a chance at fame. The few hard-working, sincere, and dedicated individuals in the film, such as Mr. Green, are humiliated and discarded.

Since politics is the "kiss of death" at the box office, few musicals explored the topic. One film musical, *Never Steal Anything Small* (1959), based on a Maxwell Anderson and Rouben Mamoulian script, documented the campaign of Jake MacIllaney (James Cagney), a waterfront labor leader, for president of the union, but it avoided any evaluative content, and its theme was simply, "Things always work out for the best."

Nothing seems to work out for the best in *Nashville*. All aspects of American life, from the "singing star" syndrome to the multi-million-dollar business of politics, are subjected to intense critical analysis. Through the platform and tactics of the "Replacement party," the director attacks both liberals and conservatives. The time for replacing the entire political system is "long past due." The Walker party can not wait to abolish the electoral college, rid Congress of lawyers, tax churches, eliminate oil and farm subsidies, and change the national anthem. *Nashville* neither advocates nor censures specific political reforms because current political and economic structures are, at best, inadequate. Robert Altman's *Nashville* thus operates on two levels: it offers a neat inversion of the traditional limits of the genre and its cynicism and disaffection define a perspective generally antithetical to traditional values of American society.

8

A Period of Frustrations

Buffalo Bill and the Indians

THE CREDITS INDICATE THAT *Buffalo Bill and the Indians, or Sitting Bull's History Lesson* is suggested by the play *Indians* by Arthur Kopit. Kopit has stated that the film contains only "about five lines"[1] from the play; some speeches survived more or less intact, such as parts of the final soliloquy of Buffalo Bill (Paul Newman).

Altman and Alan Rudolph did much more than simply shift the setting from the theater to the "real" Wild West of the screen. *Buffalo Bill and the Indians* is Altman's own version of the American myth-making process; it is a complex development of Kopit's idea of the Wild West hero. The film is a pleasure to watch on this level; the viewer is furthermore treated to performances of one of the most talented casts that Altman ever assembled. Altman gave the individuals enough leeway to create completely believable, if somewhat atypical, western personae.

The play *Indians* was a political vehicle, revealing the types of injustices suffered by American Indians at the hands of entrepreneurs. That mistreatment is an axiomatic concern in *Buffalo Bill and the Indians;* the film clearly shifts to an analysis of an American legend. The entire life of Buffalo Bill is defined in terms of his Wild West Show. The legendmaker Ned Buntline (Burt Lancaster) characterizes the show as "a pack of lies with witnesses." Bill himself sees no difference between those lies and his past; truth is "whatever gets the most applause."

The problem with *Buffalo Bill and the Indians* is that it presumes more knowledge of history than most viewers could bring to the theater. For example, Altman has Buntline mention several times that he "created" Buffalo Bill. His statements are amusing, but, without some background knowledge, it is impossible for the viewer to assess exactly what Altman is doing with this character.

In a biography of Ned Buntline, *The Great Rascal*[2] by Jay Monaghan, we learn that Buntline, whose real name was Colonel E. Z. C. Judson, went to Colorado in the summer of 1869 looking for a new hero for the dime novel he had been writing. He heard of the death of the Sioux Chief Tall Bull and decided to find the men responsible. He stumbled upon William Frederick Cody, who was young, handsome, and talkative. Although Cody was not involved in the death of Tall Bull, Buntline had found his hero.

Buntline returned to New York and began writing stories about "Buffalo Bill" (a common prairie name that he borrowed for Cody). Bill was stunned to read Buntline's accounts, but because of that notoriety Bill received various gifts (his fur coat for one) and jobs as a scout for eastern visitors. Buntline continued writing his *New York Weekly* serial, "Buffalo Bill—The King of the Border Men," which was adapted as a play by Fred Meader. Then in December 1872 Bill met his friend Buntline in Chicago, where they both starred in the play *The Scouts of the Plains,* which Buntline "borrowed" from Meader, with the addition of a temperance speech by Buntline. The show was profitable, and they soon moved it, first to St. Louis then to New York, where critics commented on "the curious grace and certain characteristic charm that please the beholder" in the performance of Buffalo Bill, who demonstrated "the utter absence of anything like stage art."

After Philadelphia, Cody decided to continue the show on his own in North Platte. Cody hired "Wild Bill" Hickok and other friends to star with him, and his show prospered. Buntline followed Cody's career through newspaper accounts, but never visited Buffalo Bill's Wild West Show. Meanwhile Bill heeded Buntline's suggestion to be remembered as a scout, not as an actor. So when Custer was killed, Cody closed the show and joined the soldiers to help "take scalps for Custer." After the capture of Sitting Bull, Cody incorporated that scene into his show and enjoyed some of the most successful seasons of his career.

Some of the liberties Altman took with the historical figures in *Buffalo Bill and the Indians* are evident. Buntline was never at the show to cause trouble for Buffalo Bill. The former partners were always friends; Bill apparently never forgot that his roots were with Buntline. Also, Buntline had assistance in "creating" Buffalo Bill, including the work of the journalist James Gordon Bennett. Although the film stands on its own as fiction, it is important to realize that the accurate historical background of the characters cannot be fully surmised or appreciated from the film alone.

Buffalo Bill and the Indians begins with a concise hypothesis of Bill's ideology—show business "ain't all that different than real life." A voice-over narration by the Old Soldier (Humphrey Gratz), the alleged "sole survivor" of Custer's Last Stand, informs the viewer that "what you are about to experience is not a show, it is a review of the down-to-earth events that made the American Frontier." The visual message is an interesting contrast to his statement. A "down-to-earth" attack on a log cabin ends abruptly when the Producer Nate Salsbury (Joel Grey) shouts, "Cease the action." The rehearsal is initially interpreted as a "real" event, and it is in this manner that Altman tricks the viewer into confusing historical "reality" and the stage action.

The film reveals a series of conflicts between Buffalo Bill and his theatrical nemesis, Chief Sitting Bull (Frank Kaquitts). Accompanied by interpreter William Halsey (Will Sampson), Sitting Bull is determined to undermine Bill's image as a star. For instance, Bill, Salsbury, and Major Burke (Kevin McCarthy) want to feature Sitting Bull in a dramatic "enactment" of Custer's Last Stand. Buffalo Bill describes his idea to Sitting Bull: "I see General George Armstrong Custer leading the courageous men of the Seventh Cavalry deep, deeper into the Indian territory known as Little Big Horn on a mission of peace, then Wham! George gets shot in the back by all the other redskins." But his rendition does not impress the chief. The chief tells Halsey to inform Buffalo Bill that he perfers another scenario—"the Sioux will have no weapons and will embrace the soldiers with open arms. Then McLaren will slaughter every man, woman, child, and dog in the village. This is what Sitting Bull has chosen to do." Annie Oakley (Geraldine Chaplin) threatens to quit if Bill fires the chief; she argues that the chief just "wants to show people the truth . . . can't [you] allow that just once?" Bill does not want to lose her act, so he begrudgingly capitulates, complaining, "I got a better sense of history than that." "History" for him consists of the interpretations of reality that he knows will draw the most fans to the Wild West Show. What is "real history" for Buffalo Bill and Nate is a "disrespect for the dead" for Sitting Bull. Even though Bill agrees that "the little bastard can stay," his confrontations with the chief escalate. President Cleveland's visit to the Wild West is marred when Sitting Bull points a loaded gun at Cleveland (Pat McCormick), and appears uninvited at the reception for the president after the show. Even after the Chief has been returned to the Standing Rock Jail to await his execution, Buffalo Bill is haunted by Sitting Bull in a dream. After Sitting Bull's death, Halsey remains at the Wild West Show to play the Chief's part in "a duel to the death." The film ends with a shot of Sitting Bull's death at Standing Rock, cross-cut with his demise in the middle of the Wild West arena.

The character of Buffalo Bill is both amusing and frightening. He can only understand others in terms of show business. He believes that Sitting Bull defies him because "you gotta look good in front of your people, just like I gotta look good in front of mine." He thinks that Custer was "a star" because "he gave the Injuns a reason to be famous." The distinction he makes between himself and Sitting Bull primarily concerns "image." As Bill sees it, "in one hundred years I'm still gonna be Buffalo Bill—star! You're still gonna be the Injun." Bill's life is full of meaning as long as he has fans. With a forceful delivery and somewhat hazy logic, Bill defends himself to the ghost of Sitting Bull: "I give them what they expect. You can't live up to what you expect, and that makes you more make-believe than me cuz you don't even know if you're bluffin'."

Bill is not the only one with this philosophy of life and entertainment. Nate believes that "we're not in the *fake* business;" he is completely outraged when McLaughlin (Denver Pyle) calls the Wild West a "circus." Frank Butler (John Considine) even manages to smile for the fans and dance from the arena after he is accidentally shot in the shoulder by his partner, Annie Oakley. Later, Burke rationalizes Sitting Bull's "escape" by saying that they are in show business, "not in the prison business." Bill's nephew Ed (Harvey Keitel) proudly remarks, "There ain't no business like the show business." Ed is later informed by the assistant producer Prentiss (Allan Nicholls) that "if he [Sitting Bull] wasn't interested in the show business he wouldn't have become a chief." Their comments perfectly capture the bizarre perspective of the Wild West Show.

In the course of their show-to-show existence, however, Bill and company must confront a series of frightening realities. As a precondition for working, Sitting Bull demands "blankets for all his people." Buffalo Bill roars, "Well now, wait a minute! What do you think this is, an army surplus store?" When Halsey somberly reveals that "there are only one hundred six Hunkpapa Sioux left at Grand River," Bill is stunned, because "five years ago we counted 10,000 braves alone." The horror of the Indians' plight is matched by the later news that McLaughlin's police had killed Sitting Bull while he was "trying to escape." Bill is faced with the cruel reality of the West but cannot and will not allow it to upset the show's routine. Bill has long been proficient at insulating himself and all of the cast from these "intrusions." He does not allow the truth to interfere with this production. When Cleveland is rude to Sitting Bull, Bill condones the insult by declaring, "You see, the difference between a President and a chief in a situation like this is a President always knows enough to retaliate before it's his turn." Interestingly, Bill's outrageous comparisons communicate an uncanny (unintended) insight into the attitudes that led to the wholesale slaughter of the American Indian. His prejudices, revealed in other racial slurs and tautologies, are representative of the way many Americans actually felt: "The difference 'tween a white man and a Injun in all situations is that a Injun is red! A Injun is red for a real good reason—so we can tell us apart!"

Bill's distortions and prejudices are detailed in a straightforward manner in the film. The satire of the western film genre is less direct. The characters' pontifications and their poses are ludicrous, but much of the film's humor is generated from Altman's attack on western clichés and the Buffalo Bill legend. Altman plays with parodies on the conventions of language barriers and the use of interpreters. Halsey prefixes his statements with "Sitting Bull says," to which Bill finally shouts, "When did he say that? He doesn't even look like he's interested." To make matters more comic, Burke becomes Buffalo Bill's interpreter, beginning his "translation" with "Halsey, what Bill means to say. . . ." Nate attempts to short-circuit the ensuing madness, yelling, "Buffalo Bill doesn't need an interpreter, Burke!" But the Major continues to obfuscate Bill's words in his attempt to be diplomatic.

The clearest example of the director's adept use of circuitous speech occurs in one of Buffalo Bill's lengthy encounters with Sitting Bull. After Halsey describes how Sitting Bull's "heart is red and sweet . . . the bears taste the honey and the green leaves lick the sky," Buffalo Bill jumps on the idiom, replying, "Halsey, you tell the chief Buffalo Bill says his leaves can turn whatever way they want, just so long as they know which way the wind's blowin'." He explains to Burke, in an aside, "I think I gave 'em the same murky logic that he gave us, what d'ya think?" His staff heartily agrees that his response was eloquent. Later Buffalo Bill glibly begins a conversation with Sitting Bull by asking, "Which way your leaves blowin'?"

Altman cleverly uses the character of Ned Buntline to undermine the very image that man created. Buntline's speech is filled with colorful, mocking analogies, succinctly delivered ("Buffalo Bill, any youngster like yourself who figures to set the world on fire best not forget where he got the matches"). Before he leaves the Wild West camp Ned proposes a toast to the star, declaring, "Buffalo Bill, [it was] the thrill of my life to have invented you." Bill's alcoholism, his failure to find the chief in the mountains, and his excuses for his impotence erode his image, but Buntline's testimony is perhaps most damning of all. The groundwork for Bill's breakdown is always present, but when Buntline departs the collapse is inevitable. The hero has been deprived of the mastermind that created him.

Buffalo Bill and the Indians is one of the few backstage, self-referential westerns in the history of cinema. It shares a show-within-a-show structure with *The Long Goodbye* and *Nashville*. The film creates a special fictional world with its own rules of logic. The people in *Buffalo Bill and the Indians*, as in *Nashville*, regard entertainment as no more than a million-dollar con game, a self-perpetuating industry, promoting images with no basis in reality. Buffalo Bill's first proposal to Sitting Bull is hilariously inappropriate—it reads like a Madison Avenue sales pitch. Bill assures Halsey, "I promise just after one season he'll never be mistaken for an average, run-of-the-mill, forgettable Injun chief; plus, he's gonna have something to fall back on in his later years."

Casting Paul Newman as Buffalo Bill adds another element of irony to

Altman recreates Buffalo Bill's Wild West show. Courtesy of United Artists, New York, NY.

the film. The Wild West is Hollywood; one can hear Newman himself speaking in Bill's comments: "It ain't easy. All my fans 're curious. It's harder being a Star than a Injun."

This film, then, was far removed from the "rousing adventure" that producer Dino de Laurentiis had expected. Altman, of course, refused to ruin the film to suit the producer. According to an infuriated de Laurentiis, "I told him [Altman], 'If you want my $7 million, you must change it the way I want.' He told me not to worry."[3] But de Laurentiis could not tamper with the film, since the director "had final cut privileges on the film's showings in the U.S., Britain, France and Canada." De Laurentiis reedited the film for its release in Germany. When the film won the Grand Prix at the Berlin Film Festival, Altman would not accept the award. He felt that De Laurentiis's cut resulted in "a version that has been edited drastically, that does not represent my work." Consequently Altman requested "that neither I nor my film be considered for any prize or honor on the basis that it perpetrated a fraud."[4]

Buffalo Bill and the Indians, unfortunately, opened and closed within two weeks in most cities in the United States in July 1976. The box-office failure probably resulted from a combination of several factors. First, United Artists did not adequately promote *Buffalo Bill*. There were very few television, newspaper, or journal ads for the film. Second, the film was released at the height of the nation's bicentennial celebration and *Buffalo Bill* ridiculed too many national traditions. The "star," Paul Newman, looked foolish. The average filmgoer, who understandably found the film "too talky," was further distanced by Altman's cynical treatment of Buffalo Bill, an American hero. Finally, as indicated, Altman assumed that the viewer was more aware of the genesis of the legend than was reasonable, which created great confusion. In a sense, the film appealed to the kind of audience that views an Off-Broadway play; it is hardly surprising that in his most recent works, Altman has turned to Off-Broadway.

Most reviewers also found the film confusing and disorganized. Andrew Sarris wrote that "nothing in Altman's Wild West is even moderately exciting or enthralling"; but then he stated, "I thoroughly respect and even grudgingly admire it for its artistic integrity."[5] Another major objection to the film was that, because Altman had replaced character interactions with ideological discussions, his characters seemed flat and there was a lack of discernible plot.

The lack of popular and critical positive response to this film is tragic, because *Buffalo Bill and the Indians* is an extremely funny, witty, and well-acted film. It contains many well-integrated subplots, each one revealing the perspective of a "peripheral" character (i.e., Annie Oakley or Buck Taylor). The humor in the film is more pointed than in *M*A*S*H* and more subtle than in *A Wedding*. The film should have been a hit. In actuality, its negative reception was the first of a series of frustrations that would plague Altman for the rest of the year.

Even before Robert Altman began production of *Buffalo Bill and the Indians*, de Laurentiis had assigned him to direct the screen version of *Ragtime*, to be filmed later. Over the objections of the producer, Altman hired Joan Tewkesbury as the screenwriter, but she eventually abandoned the project. Altman thought that "the real protagonist of *Ragtime* is the father of the immigrant family, but I think she wanted a feminist angle." Doctorow had previously refused to work on the screenplay; he "simply didn't want to relive the original writing." When Tewkesbury withdrew, Doctorow visited Altman on location at the Stoney Indian Reservation in Alberta. The novelist noticed "a sense of creative participation with cast and crew" on the set, and he changed his mind about *Ragtime*. But de Laurentiis was opposed to Doctorow as well. Altman insisted, and de Laurentiis did not interfere until he heard that Doctorow's screenplay was 390 pages long. The author was fired, and later hired as a consultant.

Meanwhile Altman was planning a six-hour, two-part version of *Ragtime*. De Laurentiis was not ready for the format and when he saw *Buffalo*

Bill and the Indians his reaction was immediate. Altman was fired from *Ragtime* one week before *Buffalo Bill and the Indians* premiered.

So prospects were bleak for the director late in the summer of 1976. Not only had he been fired from *Ragtime*, but two other projects with which he was involved were disintegrating. One was *The Yig Epoxy*, based on a concept that had fascinated Altman for at least two years. A "yig" was a specific radar mechanism on nuclear bombers; "epoxy" was a glue that held the device stable. He planned a huge-cast, big-budget black comedy centering on how this defective epoxy caused inaccurate radar sightings on the bombers. The source material was perfect for Altman— here was his chance to take on thermonuclear politics. He planned the shooting while Warner Brothers started making deals. Alan Rudolph was writing the script based on Robert Grossbach's very funny novel, *Easy and Hard Ways Out*, but the executive in charge of production for Warner Brothers, David Geffen, was very unhappy with the Rudolph screenplay. This disagreement led Altman to withdraw from the project, even though Warner Brothers had already cast Peter Falk to star in the film.

During the writing of *Buffalo Bill and the Indians*, Rudolph had also finished a screenplay of Kurt Vonnegut's *Breakfast of Champions*. Altman decided to film the work and picked up Falk, as well as Cleavon Little, Ruth Gordon, and Lily Tomlin, for the project. Sterling Hayden was cast to play the main character, Kilgore Trout. Vonnegut was impressed with the script and was in favor of the project, but a series of problems related to the acquisition of the film rights led Altman to postpone *Breakfast of Champions*, and then to abandon all hopes of producing it. According to Rudolph, "everybody got scared because it's a pretty weird movie."

While Robert Altman was toying with an untitled script of his own, Alan Rudolph finished revising a screenplay for another episodic film, *Welcome to L.A.: The City of the One-Night Stands*, based on a song by Richard Baskin. Altman agreed to produce that film, which Alan Rudolph directed. Then, from a script by Robert Benton, Altman also agreed to produce *The Late Show*, with Benton directing. These projects were the first films produced by Lion's Gate that were directed by someone other than Altman. He firmly believed that it was the responsibility of Lion's Gate to sponsor new directors who would otherwise be unable to find an outlet for their ideas, screenplays, and films.

Three Women

During this time, Altman continued writing outlines and sketches for his next film, now called *Three Women*. The idea for the film and the title, according to the director, came to him in a dream. He wrote a forty-page treatment, which was later augmented with monologues and diary entries contributed by Shelley Duvall, who was cast in the lead.

The president of Twentieth Century-Fox, Alan Ladd, Jr., agreed to finance the film. He thought that "there was a potential audience of women cool to the seemingly endless parade of films about male friendships." Altman felt that this burst of "women's films," including *Julia, The Turning Point*, and *An Unmarried Woman*, was in fact "no different from the thinking that produced black exploitation films like *Superfly*,"[6] but he accepted the offer of Ladd's studio. He cast Shelley Duvall, Sissy Spacek, and Janice Rule as Millie Lammoreaux, Pinky Rose, and Willie Hart. Production began in September 1976, with shooting in sequence and on location in Palm Springs, California, and in the desert. As usual, Altman wrote extended scenes from his treatment each evening for the next day's shooting, and dialogue was improvised during rehearsals.

Of all Altman films, *Three Women* has the skimpiest plot. As in *Images*, the film narrative gives way to characterizations of shifting psychological perspectives. Pinky emulates Millie's mannerisms, so she "becomes" Millie; Millie eventually forsakes her material concerns and adopts Willie's primitive life-style; Willie, after the stillbirth of her baby, leaves her husband, Edgar (Robert Fortier), to live with Millie and Pinky. The director offers no explanation for these *La Ronde*–like character switches.

Millie is the product and exponent of a commercial society. She believes that "the way to a man's heart is through his stomach" and posts signs in her lavender apartment saying, "Clean is sexy." Her "famous dinner party" includes Sau-Sea shrimp cocktails, pigs-in-blankets, tuna casserole, and pudding. First tolerant of Pinky, she comes to dislike her because "you don't drink, you don't smoke, you don't do anything you're supposed to do." Shelley Duvall's skill within Millie's prefabricated existence provides most of the film's humor and won her the Cannes Best Actress Award in 1977.

Pinky believes that Millie is "the most perfect person" she has ever met. She tries to match Millie's attitudes and actions, but lacks her conformist capacity. Sissy Spacek apparently attempted to incorporate aspects of her brief film career into the character of Pinky: before her "accident" she is the same innocent, gullible child as in *Badlands*, but afterwards she is the cruel, manipulative, and vengeful teenager in *Carrie*.

The most puzzling of the three women is Willie. As an artist she lives in a quiet world, but her paintings and mosaics suggest chaos and madness. She is a combination of Mattie and Keechie in *Thieves Like Us;* she is cold and detached but still suffers an intense and traumatic emotional shock. Janice Rule had a varied stage and screen background, but her role as Willie really resembled her appearance in a "Twilight Zone" episode,

Shelley Duvall as Millie and Sissy Spacek as Pinky in Three Women: *top, at a ranch, with Robert Fortier as Edgar. Courtesy of John Iltis Associates, Chicago, IL; bottom, relaxing in a deserted bar. Courtesy of John Iltis Associates, Chicago, IL.*

"Nightmare as a Child," in which she portrayed a schizophrenic who experiences hallucinations about her childhood.

Three Women works only if one pays very close attention to the meticulously drawn, exacting characterizations. The film requires the viewer to concentrate on the emotions that lead the women to abandon their individuality. It also demands that the viewer ignore gaps in its plot. Emotional involvement is also difficult because of the oblique camera approaches, the soundtrack, and the editing. First, there are too many zooms and pans focusing on objects of vague significance. Repetition dilutes the effectiveness of the zoom-ins to Pinky's horrified face as she watches Willie give birth, for example. Second, Altman uses a dramatic, upbeat, impressionistic musical score to punctuate many key shots and emotions—just as he tried to use that device in *Images* and *Quintet*. The volume-increase technique, repeated too often in *Three Women*, quickly dispels any mystery in the film. Third, the pace of the film slows to a standstill during Pinky's suicide attempt. The two-minute, special-effects sequence that communicates her frenzied mental state is of questionable aesthetic value, and could easily have been shorter.

Most reviews of *Three Women* were negative, with some critics noticing the similar topics in *Three Women* and Ingmar Bergman's *Persona*. When asked about the comparison in a 1977 interview, Altman responded that he was flattered. He also said he was "influenced" by Bergman's films.[7] This was a curious comparison, since the influence is minimal, and is noticeable in only two of his least successful films, *Images* and *Three Women*.

Twentieth Century–Fox hurried to unload *Three Women* upon the public. If there was little effort made to promote *Buffalo Bill and the Indians*, then there was absolutely no time or energy spent advertising *Three Women*. The film opened and closed across the country within a few weeks. Since it cost only $1.6 million to make, there was a small profit for the director and producer, but not enough to match distribution costs for Fox. No plans were made for another release for *Three Women*. It was sold to Films Incorporated for nontheatrical showings.

Robert Altman obviously was not having much luck after *Nashville*. Many projects besides *Ragtime*, *The Yig Epoxy*, and *Breakfast of Champions* were planned but either discarded or postponed indefinitely. The times were disappointing; but perhaps it was frustration that encouraged him to jump into his next project—a comedy of the absurdities in upper-class American culture—which would occupy him for the next eight months.

9

Success and Experimentation

WHILE HE WAS COMPLETING *Three Women* in Palm Springs early in 1977 Altman was asked what he planned to film next. He answered sarcastically that he always wanted to photograph a wedding. Over lunch he discussed the idea with Scottie Bushnell and others. That evening he wrote an outline and began collaborating with John Considine on a story.

A Wedding

For *A Wedding*, Altman began one of the most extensive and detailed preproduction periods of his career. This film was to be totally different from *Three Women*. He classified it with "*Nashville* and *M*A*S*H* and that group of films"[1] because it had forty-eight major characters. He intended to handle the mammoth casting task with the help of Dennis Hill and Scottie Bushnell.

Altman first decided to feature Sissy Spacek and Shelly Duvall in the film but Spacek "walked out of the film without telling me."[2] Shelly Duvall agreed to work on the film, but suddenly she, too, decided to withdraw. She was romantically involved with Paul Simon, who opposed the project. There was also speculation that Duvall was "afraid of being type-cast as an Altman contract player." She departed while he was in Chicago, scouting locations and auditioning actors for the film. While waiting to recast these roles, Altman started working on other parts. His first idea for Mrs. Tulip Brenner was Dinah Shore, but Shore failed to respond to his offers. He was soon contacted by Carol Burnett's agent, who told him she would love to do the film. Altman called Burnett who immediately accepted the part without seeing the script "because it was Robert Altman. I had heard from several people, including Lily Tomlin, that he was one of the greatest people in the world to work for."

To obtain Vittorio Gassman's services, Altman flew to Italy and convinced him to take the part by simply describing the intriguing background of Luigi Corelli. The role of the drunken and lecherous Dr. Meecham went to Howard Duff, to whom Altman explained, "You've

Extraordinary moments of revelation: top, A Wedding.
Courtesy of Lion's Gate Films, Westwood, CA; bottom,
Quintet. *Courtesy of Films Incorporated, Wilmette, IL.*

been studying for this part for years. Now you can finally do it." Dina Merrill, who played Antoinette Sloan Godard, the groom's aunt, received the part becaused she asked her friend Bert Remsen to see if there was a role available for her. Viveca Lindfors, who played the cateress Ingrid Hellstrom, had previously written to Altman expressing her eagerness to work with him. Lauren Hutton admitted that she received the part of Flo Farmer, the film producer, "on the casting couch." She explained that she went to Lion's Gate, sat on a couch and told the director that she was "not leaving here til you find a part for me. I don't care how small it is."[3]

Actors who had previously worked with Altman, including Geraldine Chaplin, John Cromwell, Nina Van Pallandt, Pat McCormick, Ruth Nelson, John Considine, and Bert Remsen, were given prominent roles in the film. Most members of the cast were, therefore, signed before Altman had decided who would play the bride, the role Sissy Spacek had refused. The choice presented some problems for Altman. He had planned to hire Leslie Rogers after an audition, but later he felt she was not quite right for the part. Rogers suggested Amy Stryker, who visited Altman at the Oak Park, Illinois, set. After a twenty-minute talk, in which Altman inquired about her feelings on country music, weddings, and other topics, he offered her the part. The fact that she wore dental braces was a decisive factor. Altman explained that he would never have forced an actress to wear braces for the role, but since she was already wearing them, he felt that this would provide a naturally comic touch. Stryker described Muffin as "a naive, young thing . . . her whole life was geared to her wedding, her goal."[4]

After settling on the cast, finding locations in Oak Park and Lake Forest, Illinois, and trying to promote *Three Women* across the country, Altman went to the Cannes Film Festival. He expressed complete confidence that his staff would continue to work efficiently on *A Wedding's* preproduction details while he was gone: "My staff knows what I want better than I do. If I'm there, they feel like they have to check with me, and that only slows them down."[5]

He began shooting the $4 million Twentieth Century Fox Film on 15 June at the Grace Episcopal Church in Oak Park. Because *A Wedding* was to be shot in sequence, several complications arose. The Episcopalian pastor agreed to the use of the church only for a few days, so the wedding ceremony had to be filmed quickly. Altman needed to finish shooting the entire film by 10 August at the latest because Carol Burnett had to begin television work. Most importantly, the mansion of Mrs. Aleka Armour in Lake Forest, which was the home of the groom's family in the film, was available only until mid-August and only if they contributed to her favorite charity. A $40,000 fee was promptly donated to the Rehabilitation Institute of Illinois. Altman also promised that the world premiere of the film

Altman discusses the church scene with Carol Burnett in A Wedding. *Courtesy of Lion's Gate Films, Westwood, CA.*

would be held in Chicago for the benefit of the Rehabilitation Institute.[6] Everything seemed to be falling in place for Altman.

From 15 to 18 June, Altman shot the church ceremony. In the face of pressing needs for speed and efficiency, he kept the cast and crew in good spirits. Their easy rapport was apparent from the first day of shooting, with Altman confident, joking with his assistant Tommy Thompson. Amy Stryker recalled that one day the air conditioner in the church failed so the cast members went outside "to talk, relax, play frisbee. Then Bob came outside and said, 'Excuse me, but would you come back inside so we can continue shooting?' in a very nice tone. [He was] warm and wonderful to work for." The rest of the cast felt similarly, and church shooting was rapidly completed. Then the cast was relocated to the Sheraton in Waukegan, Illinois, for the rest of the film. Shooting at the mansion began five days later. The television program "60 Minutes" interviewed the cast for a segment airing in January of the following year in which Mike Wallace insinuated that the filming was an eight-week free-for-all, an alcohol and drugs debacle. The cast and director denied such allegations. Carol

Burnett described the group experience as a wholesome, happy, "Saturday matinee family atmosphere." Others agreed that warmth and friendship were shared in the undertaking even under time and budget constraints.

The loose style to which Wallace objected was no more or less extreme than in any other Altman project. For example, improvisations from the 150-page script occurred within rehearsal, and cast members were given their lines the night before shooting. Altman also gave each actor a "secret" about their background. Muffin (Amy Stryker) was formerly a cheerleader whose favorite player was her husband-to-be, Dino (Desi Arnaz, Jr.); her sister Buffy (Mia Farrow) was pregnant with Dino's child; Regina Corelli (Nina Van Pallandt) was a girlfriend of Castro and a morphine addict; and Tulip planned an assignation with the groom's uncle (Pat McCormick). In a master stroke of casting, Altman convinced Lillian Gish to return to acting as the grandmother Nettie (named after Altman's grandmother). Nettie dies during the wedding ceremony and thus becomes the "secret" over which the family and friends keep stumbling throughout the reception.

The wedding involves two rich families. The bride's family, the Brenners, have recently acquired their wealth (operating a truckstop in Louisville), while those on the groom's side, the Corellis, live in Lake Bluff, Illinois, and are considered an "old money" family. The plot of the film is simple. Dino Corelli and Muffin Brenner get married. The groom's family holds the reception, but only one guest (Bert Remsen) arrives at their home, and he insults everyone in the reception line. Given the difficulties they will encounter, even one guest is more trouble than the Corellis and Brenners can handle. The reception is interrupted by several deaths, sexual liaisons, arguments, and even a tornado, each affecting the lives of the participants in significant ways.

The dependence on characterization in *A Wedding* is greater than in *Nashville*, but the viewer never feels confident about any particular character. Additional background information, new clues, and much innuendo are continually injected into the film. The viewer does not learn until the end of the film, for example, that the Brenners have a yearly income of over $5 million and are not in fact "country hicks." Luigi Corelli's appearance and actions suggest an ominous "Godfather" presence, an assumption that is not repudiated until the end of the film. The large number of characters creates confusion about the exact identity of any of them, as though the viewer were another guest of the family's, rather than a passive observer. Acceptance or rejection of a particular character is guided by emotional reactions and new information, rather than intellectualization—an ideal Altman had in mind since *Images*. Actions of the characters always "capture" the occasion. Rita Billingsley (Geraldine Chaplin), the coordinator of the wedding, tells a servant, "This isn't a circus, it's a wedding!" The reprimand becomes the credo for the orchestrated chaos of the day. The logic of the event is indeed skewed. A security force, hired to help the Corellis avoid any disturbances, ends up assaulting Luigi's brother, who is mistaken for a burglar. Jeff Kuykendall (John Considine), the security chief, tells his assistant on a two-way radio, "I'm in control here," but their "technology" and the fight that they start turn that wedding into a circus. The bride's father, Snooks (Paul Dooley), when informed about Buffy's pregnancy, screams, "You can't lie about a thing like this—it's too big!" His reaction describes the director's attitude toward his subject. The artificiality and pretensions in both the nouveau riche and the old-money families are equally ludicrous and far too huge to pass unnoticed. *A Wedding* is one of the few films on the American upper class to approach the same level of satire that *The Rules of the Game* did with French society.

The benefit premiere in Chicago in April 1978 was risky since the film was scheduled for an October release. Altman claimed that "it's undoubtedly going to hurt us. Delays are usually interpreted as meaning there's something wrong with the film." For once his fears were inaccurate. *A Wedding*'s premiere was "a complete success,"[7] and when the film opened in New York, Los Angeles, and Chicago in September 1978, it was well attended. The film had been given nationwide advertising, and it was selected as the opening-night entry for the New York Film Festival. *A Wedding* was listed in the 8 November 1978 issue of *Variety* as the ninth biggest money-maker in October. It ran for nearly four months—in New York—the longest run of any previous Altman film except *M*A*S*H* and *Nashville*. Enjoying its commercial success, Altman quipped, "I'm not doing weddings any more—I'm doing more serious things now." By this time Altman was receiving consistent critical support. Vincent Canby called him one of the most prolific film artists in the business. Andrew Sarris identified a new group of "dissonant directors" who "go against the grain of sentimental expectation." In that category "Altman, Huston, Kubrick, and Lester come closer to Pantheon caliber than others."[8]

While he was waiting for the release of *A Wedding*, Altman began outlining, writing, filming, and editing two new projects: *Quintet* and *A Romance* (later called *A Perfect Couple*). He was also producing two films, Alan Rudolph's *Remember My Name* and Rich Young's *Rich Kids*, and writing a treatment for the film *Health*. He speculated that "maybe I'm doing all this so I can get a lot done before they catch up to me."[9]

Quintet

Quintet was a film that certainly went "against the grain" of popular and critical expectation. The film ran in major cities for a week with little or no advance publicity by Twentieth Century–Fox and was panned by most critics. Canby qualified his charge that *Quintet* was "the most aggressively indulgent motion picture made in the last twenty years by a major American director" by stating, "I continue to hope that Mr. Altman won't listen to us critics and to hope that he'll continue to make exactly the sort of film he wants to,"[10] which describes exactly what Altman did before, during, and after *Quintet*.

Quintet describes "the death of a culture," and the claustrophobia and despair in it recall the tone of *Thieves Like Us*. The protagonist of *Quintet* resembles Marlowe in *The Long Goodbye*. Altman was not sure what inspired the film. He and story-writers Lionel Chetwynd and Patricia Resnick thought it was "a project I talked about five or six years ago." Altman stated, "My father was dying of cancer at the time . . . that event and the experience had a great deal to do with the ultimate drift of the film."[11]

Altman desired a bleak visual appearance for *Quintet*. He adapted still-photograph camera filters to the 35mm Panavision cameras that his cinematographer Jean Boffety (*Thieves*) used. This invention, along with the use of conventional diffusion filters, resulted in a circular deep-focus or "iris focus" area in center screen, with the frame's outer circumference blurred, highlighting the hero in his struggle for survival in an arctic world. Altman did not equate a bleak visual style with impoverished mise-en-scène. He hoped to combine beautiful frozen landscapes with detailed interior shots of a dying civilization, much like the Los Angeles later seen in Ridley Scott's *Blade Runner* (1982).

Altman wanted a "Carol Reed thriller" set in the future after an ice age. He was "guaranteed" sufficient snow and ice if he shot the film in Canada, north of Montreal. He scouted locations there and in the Arctic Circle, and began set construction near Montreal, with the help of production designer Leon Erickson. Scottie Bushnell assisted at this stage by designing costumes for the cast.

The director approached Fernando Rey, Vittorio Gassman, Bibi Andersson, Paul Newman, and others to act in a film for him. Without seeing a script or knowing anything about the film, they accepted. The film's $7 million budget was spent mostly on the stars' salaries and on "the magnitude of the sets, and the difficulties of location shooting."

Frank Barhydt helped Altman write parts of a *Quintet* screenplay, but the director and cast worked in sequence without a script per se, the cast learning its lines before the following day's shooting. Fernando Rey described how Altman "had a *general* idea of what he was doing, but in the way you were acting, you gave him an idea on how to go on." Rey felt that this relaxed method was similar to that of Luis Buñuel: "They don't try to explain everything. Bob works to express himself in a surrealistic way. Like Buñuel, he is a great poet."[12]

The plot of the film is more complex than one could hope to follow in a first viewing. The story begins with Essex (Paul Newman) and Vivia (Bridgette Fossey) walking across a barren, frozen landscape. They seem tired but happy. When they stop to rest, the scene quickly cuts to Grigor (Fernando Rey) standing in a large casino. He informs six people that they will play in some sort of tournament, and he gives each person a list with five names on it.

Then a complicated chain of events begins to unfold. Essex and Vivia visit Francha (Tom Hill), the brother of Essex. (Francha was one of the men in the tournament.) Essex leaves to purchase some firewood, and while he is gone Francha and his guests play a mysterious dice game (devised by Altman) called quintet. Before Essex returns, a bomb explodes, killing Vivia and his brother. Essex later spots the killer, Redstone (David Langton), and chases him, but Redstone is killed by a third member of the tournament who is named St. Christopher (Vittorio Gassman). Essex eventually finds the list that Redstone was given in the casino, and he decides to assume Redstone's identity. He also learns that Redstone lived at the Hotel Electra, and so he goes there to unravel the mystery of his brother's death. At the hotel he meets Deuca (Nina Van Pallandt) and Ambrosia (Bibi Andersson), two women whose names he recognizes from Redstone's list. Grigor mentions that he is the tournament judge, but he plays along with Essex's assumed identity, telling him in a "knowing" manner, "I knew you were a player. I saw that fire in your eyes. Only tournament players have that sense of life."

Essex plays quintet with Deuca and Ambrosia, and is, theoretically, "killed with one throw" of the dice. He later observes Gladstar (Craig Nelson), whose name was on his list, talking to Ambrosia, threatening the life of St. Christopher. Essex thus concludes that those people on his list will all eventually die. To confirm his suspicion he must return to his brother's apartment to compare Francha's list with Redstone's. Meanwhile Deuca kills Gladstar, and St. Christopher kills her. St. Christopher and Ambrosia follow Essex. St. Christopher falls through some ice and is impaled on his spear; Essex slays Ambrosia, carries her body back to the judge, and departs from the city forever, an outsider returning to his natural environment, like Shane returning to the mountains.

As Essex, Paul Newman plays a part directly opposite his Buffalo Bill Cody portrayal. Essex looks for "understanding," "education," and "hope." Altman called Essex Everyman, but the character resembles Marlowe gone north, tracking down another killer, running into some bad weather, bad luck, and a crooked dice game. Essex is reflective, and he consciously resists all attempts to infringe upon his personal code of honor. He refuses to become "the greatest player of them all" in the newest cultural pastime—murder. He kills only once, to save his own life.

Essex combats death "on all levels" against three individuals: Grigor, St. Christopher, and Ambrosia. His main opponent is the Mephistopholean Grigor, who runs the frozen world and "judges" quintet tournaments. Essex also battles the religious fervor St. Christopher brings to the game. Altman establishes a particularly lunatic personality and life-style for this character. When Christopher is not killing players or mumbling prayers in Latin, he is conducting Salvation Army gatherings, consisting of a period of "solace" before the soup line forms. His "solace" is a lecture on "the finality of death," what all men "have to look forward to," and why their "wretched lives are supremely happy." During the lecture he tells his following that "life is an interruption of the void . . . to be cherished" only moments before he kills Deuca by shoving a dagger through her skull. Grigor and St. Christopher conspire against Essex. They also underestimate him: it is, therefore, "a surprise, but not a coincidence" when Chistopher appears at the same bar to which Grigor had brought Essex.

Essex also faces death in the guise of beauty. While in bed with Ambrosia, he is told that she "never thinks of the past," that he reminds her "of what we lost," and that "death is arbitrary." Her words and actions seem real, but they are all an act. Intending to kill Essex, she tells Grigor that she is "supremely content" with the progress of the tournament. She readily accepts her own death, which further illustrates that the *Quintet* civilization cannot sustain any new ideas about life or love. Essex's offspring and his lovers die, which is fortunate, since Fox would have never touched *Quintet II*.

The struggle to overcome his opponents is reflected in the visual imagery of the film. His strength of will is indicated by a number of close-ups on a single light bulb in his frozen hotel room. When Essex turns the switch, the bulb radiates heat and melts the ice-enclosed fixture and wall. The light bulb and the fires in *Quintet* are overly simplistic metaphors for Essex's resilience to a hostile environment.

The game itself is also an overworked metaphor. Deuca says that the dice game is a front game, which the viewer already suspects. Quintet involves a "killing order" that foreshadows the sequence of deaths in the film. The sixth man in the game "has the advantage," and Essex becomes the sixth man when Redstone dies. When the characters mention "the tournament" they are referring to their own end-game, not to the game of dice. So the information Altman supplies about the game is filled with "meaningful" specifics but lacks a general rationale.

Tom Pierson's musical score is used to foreshadow violence, but again it is heavy-handed. The arrangements often build from piano solos to full orchestration simulating the booming crescendo of an avalanche. That sound is employed throughout the film as a death-throe. First paired with Essex, then with the tournament players, it finally is directly linked to St.

Christopher at the moment of his death. Sound does not "punctuate" the action, as in *Three Women;* here it underlines the suspense.

Ultimately, Essex is victorious over the game because, despite its bleakness and depression, *Quintet* is supposedly a celebration of "life-force." He alone survives the inertia, the philosophical traps, and the attempts on his life. The reassuring ending in particular made critics question the premise of *Quintet.* Vincent Canby sarcastically complimented the film for "those beautiful woolen stoles" everyone wore in the picture. Critics also noted that the mechanics of the game were never satisfactorily explained, although this vagueness was consistent with Altman's existential theme, that the rules of life are by themselves unimportant.

Much of the film depends on Altman's ability to maintain suspense. It works well for him in one scene when a bomb explodes in the apartment of Essex's brother. Nevertheless, this type of suspense is not Altman's forte to begin with, and the leaden script kills off viewer interest at key moments. Lines such as "To understand the scheme you must be part of the scheme, yes, at the exact moment it is too late" do not add much to the drama, or the sense, of the film. There are in fact so many elements at odds in *Quintet* that one wonders where Altman went wrong with the film. The philosophy espoused is trite, but the problem is deeper than that. The viewer is left with the impression that Altman never really believes in any of the existential rhetoric in the fatal parchesi game his characters are playing.

A Perfect Couple

While editing *Quintet* late in 1978 Altman began production of *A Perfect Couple,* abruptly changing from a metaphoric melodrama to a light love comedy. *A Perfect Couple,* a relatively minor film, describes the romantic relationship between conservative businessman Alex Theodopoulos (Paul Dooley) and his young hippie girlfriend Sheila Shea (Marta Heflin), whom he meets through a video computer-dating service. They immediately fall in love, but because of their different ages and cultural backgrounds the relationship is stormy. For example, Sheila sings with a rock band called Keepin' 'Em off the Streets, while Alex prefers the Los Angeles Philharmonic. Several fights about her communal living arrangements ensue. Alex objects to her friends and her freewheeling philosophy of life, while Sheila has difficulty adjusting to his family and accepting their traditional notions of employment and marriage. Humor is supposed to emerge from the differences in their backgrounds, but most of it is pathos: Alex standing out in the rain; Alex brow-beaten by his father; or Sheila's temper tantrums.

Paul Dooley as Alex and Marta Heflin as Sheila, the oddly matched "perfect couple."
Courtesy of Films Incorporated, Wilmette, IL.

The film is pleasant to watch, if one overlooks Heflin's terrible performance. Written by Altman and Allan Nicholls, it is at least a cheerful break
from the death and despair of *Quintet,* yet it illustrates many of the same
problems of the previous film. There really is no apparent plot; the script
is impoverished; and the motivation is obscure. Like *Quintet, A Perfect
Couple* does not demonstrate any thorough, believable, or important
thesis.

As was the case with *Quintet, A Perfect Couple* had a minimal promotion effort and an attenuated release. Audience response was not positive
where it was screened, and the film was mostly ignored by critics. Meanwhile, early in 1979, Altman was expanding his Lion's Gate corporation in
Westwood. Two sound stages, with capacities for sound effects, dialogue,
music recording, and remixing, were completed. The stages also served
as fifty-seat theaters, and an additional screening room was built. The film
complex was scheduled for completion late in the fall of that year. Altman
named Tommy Thompson and Robert Eggenweiler as president and vice-
president of the corporation.

Health

With "firmed commitments to direct through 1981,"[13] Altman next began production of his screenplay *Health* on location at the Don Cesar
Beach Hotel in St. Petersburg, Florida. Produced and directed by Altman, through Lion's Gate and Twentieth Century–Fox, *Health* is "another
of the *Nashville-Wedding-M*A*S*H* kind of large-arena films." It stars
James Garner, Carol Burnett, Lauren Bacall, Glenda Jackson, Paul Dooley, Henry Gibson, and three-dozen other actors, and is set at a national
health-industry convention. Its title is an acronym for the convention slo-
gan, "Happiness, energy, and longevity through health." At the convention, Esther Brill (Lauren Bacall), an eighty-three-year-old virgin and
health devotee, and Isabella Garnell (Glenda Jackson), who borrows
speeches from Adlai Stevenson, are opposing candidates for the presiden-
cy of the industry. The plot describes the espionage, deceit, fights, and
assassination that figure into the campaign, while Dick Cavett, playing
himself, reports on the activities. The treatment of politics in the film is at
times serious and metaphorical. On other occasions, the general approach
is as outrageous as it is in *Brewster McCloud*—Altman dresses cast members as a stalk of celery, an avocado, and even as a tomato, whom he shows
drowning in a swimming pool.

Health was certainly a major improvement over his two previous films.
Shot in sequence over a three-month period, the film evidences a remarkable coordination of cast members. The script, pace, and editing are surprisingly captivating for such a long, essayistic film. In many ways, *Health*
is a humorous companion piece to *Nashville*. Like John Triplette in *Nashville*, salesman Harold Gainey (Paul Dooley) moves through the industry
promoting his nonsensical product (powdered kelp, which he calls "Vita-
Sea"). The songs of the vaudeville group The Steinettes provide some
ironic commentary on the health crisis implied in the film, just as the
songs in *Nashville* capture the cynicism about politics and the music
industry.

Health contains some great qualities of Altman filmmaking, primarily
because he is dealing with his favorite subject, contemporary American
culture, in an extremely relaxed, loose, and funny manner. In one scene,
for example, a presidential representative named Gloria Burbank (Carol
Burnett) discovers a body at the bottom of a swimming pool, but the
"corpse" turns out to be "Gill" Gainey, breathing through a hidden oxygen
tank, hoping to get some publicity when his body is discovered. Later
Gloria awakens her ex-husband Harry Wolff (James Garner) in the middle
of the night to describe a right-wing extremist contingent that she believes
is operating in the industry. The viewer recognizes the significance of her
statement, but because the editing is quick and her manner is hysterical,

A sardonic Harry Wolff (James Garner) once again resuscitates Esther Brill (Lauren Bacall). Courtesy of Films Incorporated, Wilmette, IL.

her theory loses credibility. The viewer sides with Harry largely because he is calm, rational, and well-meaning enough. The viewer knows that some of her charges are accurate, yet the sensible, realistic approach of Harry ("the government isn't going to topple overnight") is still preferable. Logic is no longer operative, and the strange events in *Health* occur too quickly to permit second-guessing. There are no easy solutions to the predicaments of the characters. The events are crazy, but the conventioneers are not aware of anything being amiss. The viewer identifies with Harry, who seems to be the only person able to keep things in perspective. When questioned about the Health candidates and the election, Harry explains "When you're that crazy, everyone listens to you." The actions and words in *Health* are so ambiguous that, although Altman is not intentionally confusing the audience, his tale is not completely forthright. Without question, the best feature of the film is James Garner's performance. His expressions of disbelief, his jokes and comments ("Hi, Colonel!" to a security guard dressed as an ear of corn), his sarcastic treatment of Gainey ("Why don't you go hold your breath?"), and his generally unpretentious manner help the viewer appreciate the problems of confronting deluded politicians, messianic salesmen, and talking vegetables. *Health* certainly deserved mass marketing and a large promotion campaign. After *Quintet* and *A Perfect Couple*, however, Fox was reluctant to make any expenditures on Altman's work. They refused to distribute the film. The politics of the situation so infuriated Altman that he personally took *Health* to several film festivals. The exposure and the prizes that it gathered in Venice and Montreal persuaded Fox (then under the management of Norman Levy) to try it in Los Angeles. *Health* played in Westwood for a few weeks and was well attended. It was then withdrawn, with no further plans for distribution. Altman believed that the film was being dumped because it was made when Alan Ladd, Jr., was still in charge, before Fox became interested only in big profits, skiing interests in Aspen, and Coca-Cola. But Levy claimed that the film was something the public did not want to buy. Had *Health* been well publicized and released properly (at a probable expenditure of $2 million), in all likelihood it would have done as well as *A Wedding*. *Health* had a limited cable-television play before it was sold to CBS for a nationwide television showing in August 1983.

The difficulties with the release of *Health* were exacerbated because Altman was in Malta most of the time preparing for *Popeye*. This film, based on a Jules Feiffer screenplay, became Altman's biggest commercial success since *M*A*S*H*, and it was a film that, for once, was certain to be promoted properly.

10

Popeye

POPEYE HAS TO BE the Robert Altman film that best displays his ability to create a world of fantasy—a completely enclosed universe for his characters to inhabit—and his uncanny talent for casting the actors that most naturally fit into that existence. *Popeye* also has some of the finest characterizations Altman ever developed to complement his casting. It is the most carefully planned, intricately detailed, and perfectly set of all his films. The use of songs, multi-leveled, simultaneous dialogue, brilliant asides, and sardonic, ever-present mumblings of the title character communicates an aural richness rivaling the quality of sound in *Nashville* and *California Split*. With the constant commentary of a main character—whose tone ranges from sincerity to quick sarcasm—Altman reveals Popeye's own attitudes toward life. The soundtrack thematically and emotionally reinforces the poetic charm, struggles, and contradictions of the world of Sweethaven.

For all its quaintness, Sweethaven is a microcosm of conservative American society—only "a little more bizarre than Cleveland."[1] It is into this staid, controlled existence that the hero wanders. Popeye has an ideological perspective that is foreign to the townspeople. He has an unshaking commitment to honesty, individualism, and self-reliance and in general he possesses an uncompromising set of moral guidelines. For Popeye, "wrong is wrong, even when it helps ya." He tells Bluto outright, "Even though you're larger than me, you can't win, 'cuz you're bad and the good always wins over the bad." Popeye is a wonderfully humorous character and verbal wit is a large part of his appeal. The wordplay in *Popeye* is more outrageous than in any other Altman film. Robert Altman and Jules Feiffer do not hesitate to use corny lines: "I ain't no doctor, but I know when I'm losin' me patience" or "Burgers can't be choosers" (Wimpy admiring a soupburger). The town of Sweethaven is filled with puns. A "floating" boxing match is held on "Max and Sons Square Garden," and Scab Island, where the treasure is buried, is described as "the rock—it's a

Robin Williams brings Popeye to life: top, *with Olive Oyl (Shelley Duvall) and Wimpy (Paul Dooley);* bottom, *battling Bluto (Paul L. Smith) in the finale. Courtesy of Paramount Pictures/Walt Disney Productions, Los Angeles, CA.*

117

hard place." *Popeye* uses some of the most laughable "mispronunskiations" since Inspector Clouseau.

The live sound, the dialogue, and the interactions of the characters create a surreal, comic-strip world. Despite the arguments and fights, Sweethaven is a place where Popeye can catch a piano in midair and fight an octopus with the help of some spinach.

Origins of the Film

The qualities that make *Popeye* work so well—casting, acting, use of sound, staging, and cinematography—are the same qualities that make the film difficult to categorize. Discussing his hopes for *Popeye*, Altman said, "As a filmmaker, I am thrilled with the idea of having access to the Disney audience, which I have always been trying to reach," but the film is no more a simple, live-action cartoon for children than it is a love story, a musical, or a political commentary. *Popeye* attempts, more than any other of his films (except *M*A*S*H*), to reach viewers on several different levels. In that regard, Altman has eclipsed his expectations; the film has already grossed nearly $50 million.

In order to understand how the film works, and how difficulties in the film jeopardize its artistic integrity, one must carefully examine the origins, the production techniques, the contributions of the actors, and the narrative. Robert Evans began with the idea for *Popeye* and worked on a coproduction deal between his studio (Paramount) and Walt Disney Productions. Evans first cast Dustin Hoffman, who had starred in Evans's *Marathon Man*, in the title role. Following a suggestion of his executive producer, Richard Sylbert, he offered Jules Feiffer the screenwriter's job, which Feiffer accepted on the condition that he could base the scenario on the E. C. Segar comic strip, not on the animated cartoon character of the 1950s. Evans then started looking for a director. His first choice was Hal Ashby, who was unavailable. At the same time, Robert Altman had received a copy of the script from Sam Cohn. He read it and liked it. Evans proposed Altman's name to Paramount but the studio did not share his enthusiasm for Altman. Evans faced a struggle, but eventually hired Altman over more commercial directors like Mike Nichols or Arthur Penn, whom Paramount had preferred.

In the meantime, because of some script problems, Dustin Hoffman left the project. It is difficult to determine exactly who proposed Robin Williams as Popeye, but it is certain that Williams did not begin serious preparation for the role until Altman was in charge. Williams lost twenty pounds, began boxing, took tapdance lessons, and developed a voice that sounded to him "as if I gargled with Liquid Wrench." Feiffer developed Popeye as "the only honest man in a world filled with adorable thieves."

He also wanted to show all characters in conflict, with "unity through fighting"—Popeye arguing with Olive and fighting Spike, Butch, Mort, the Taxman, the Commodore, and Bluto.

Then Altman called Shelley Duvall and cast her as Olive Oyl, skipping over Lily Tomlin and Gilda Radner. Duvall had finished filming *The Shining*, and flew to Malta, the island that Altman had selected for the setting because of its perfect climate. He also found Malta appealing because it was far from Hollywood and he was already concerned about losing control, since he was not producer of the film.

Upon her arrival Duvall began struggling with cork-filled boots, size 14 quadruple-A. She put on a three-piece wig, and soon she became "a combination of Stan Laurel and Mae West." After a great deal of debate, the director settled on Harry Nilsson for the music, cast Paul L. Smith as Bluto, and, in what proved to be a perfect selection, found Paul Dooley for Wimpy. The role of Mrs. Oxheart went to Linda Hunt, who later starred in *The Year of Living Dangerously*, directed by Peter Weir, whose films Altman greatly admires. Altman used the Steinettes from *Health* as the pitiful Wallfleur Sisters, who assist Olive. He also used Allan Nicholls for the seventh time, giving him the role of Rough House. Another Altman veteran, from *McCabe and Mrs. Miller* and *Three Women*, was Robert Fortier, who played Bill Barnacle. Two of the musicians in the film were actually accomplished performers, Van Dyke Parks and Klaus Voorman. The choice for Swee' Pea was significant for Altman: he decided to use his one-year-old grandson to play the part.

The construction of Sweethaven, with forty houses, a church, sunken ships, a fire station, and a café, costing nearly $2 million, began in October 1979 under the supervision of Robert Eggenweiller, C. O. Erickson, and Wolf Kroeger. The twenty-week shooting in Malta was another "Altman community experience" for cast and crew. Altman wanted the cast to feel like family, so there were regular social activities, dinners, and screenings of the rushes and films made by Allan Rudolph, Robert Benton, Robert Altman, Walt Disney, and Guisseppe Rotunno. The only personality conflicts that arose during the shooting were those between Robert Altman and Jules Feiffer, Robin Williams and Jules Feiffer, and Harry Nilsson and Jules Feiffer. Evans was called in a few times as an intermediary; eventually Jules Feiffer recognized that "what he [Robert Altman] is doing adds immeasurably to all the things I wanted the film to be—with that sense of orchestration and of things unwinding, casually and accidentally instead of tightly plotted." Altman worked harder on this film than he had in many years, with more rehearsals and longer daily shooting. Although they still went well over the $13.6 million budget, he was able to keep everyone relaxed, confident, and encouraged. He set up an atmosphere in which everyone felt as though they were involved in creating something magical and fun. As in the past, this sense of ease and confidence enabled each actor to experiment, add dialogue, and develop mannerisms that made each character unique and more appealing. With these personalities, struggles, and affinities, Altman shaped character "silhouettes" into a film that is "not a weird movie about strange people doing strange things, but essentially a nice movie with Altman's colors in it."²

Story Line

Robert Altman immediately informs the viewer that the character of Popeye in the film differs from the Fleischer cartoon creation. The film opens with the Popeye theme song, and immediately the cartoon figure appears in a mid-screen inset, saying, "Hey, what's this? One of Bluto's tricks? I'm in the wrong movie!" This comic introduction, like the one in *Nashville*, tells the slightly disoriented viewer to forget expectations and give in to what follows. Visually it also reminds the viewer of the real difference between the cartoon Popeye and the one that appears in the movie. The effectiveness of Altman stylistics and characterization is equally apparent in two subsequent scenes: Popeye's entrance to Sweethaven and his fight at the Roughhouse Café on the next day.

After the cartoon, the director cuts to a long shot of Popeye rowing his dinghy in a storm. The thunder abates as the craft approaches land, and we hear a church bell ringing. When the bell stops, dawn breaks on cue, and the first song, "Sweethaven," begins as Wimpy walks out of the house of Nana Oyl (Roberta Maxwell) toward the café. The sudden dawn, the sets, costuming, and the orchestrated madness of the people of Sweethaven setting about their daily chores quickly establish the town as a nonstop, comic-strip world that Popeye enters. He is immediately accosted by the Taxman (Donald Moffat), who threatens Popeye with scores of fines, including a "nickel question tax," and by Geezil, who will sell broccoli or spinach to Popeye when he wants carrots. Popeye's casual acceptance of the town is revealed in his song "Blow Me Down." As he walks through town looking for a "room to renk," he is nearly smashed by a falling piano and is knocked down by the Roughhouse gang. But he takes it all in stride, singing how "wherever I go, I yam wot I yam, that does it for me." The camera movement is fluid throughout the sequence, quickly immersing this outsider in the mainstream of Sweethaven life. Popeye's uniqueness is also revealed by posing him next to Olive Oyl. The first view of Olive is shocking. Her black, red, and white blouse and skirt make Popeye look more earthy. Her incessant cackling, her clumsiness, and her defensiveness accentuate Popeye's easygoing nature and make his habit of disguising sarcastic remarks (by mumbling them) even more appealing.

The viewer is further drawn to accept the perspective of Popeye because everyone else in the Oyl house is absolutely irrational. Wimpy is obsessed with food. Cole Oyl has a constant need to receive apologies from everyone. Castor Oyl will only discuss the price of gold and fish futures, that is, until he interrupts Olive's ravings, yelling at her, "No one can stop me from agreeing with you if I want to!" It is impossible for Popeye to eat dinner in this madhouse, so the viewer feels quite comfortable with him when he goes up to his room. His desire to find his father seems to be the only reasonable request in the house. When he kisses the empty picture frame (upon which he has printed "me poppa") goodnight, the viewer finds him "strange" but nice.

The next day all the people of Sweethaven, with Wimpy in the lead, head toward the Roughhouse Café. This entertaining, well-choreographed sequence is the culmination of the first part of the film, which introduces Popeye and the viewer to Sweethaven culture. Hilarious visuals are linked to the lyrics of Wimpy's theme song, "Everything is food." For example, Wimpy grabs another hamburger from Swifty, the cook (Carlo Pellegrini), as he sings his famous line, "I would gladly pay you Tuesday for a hamburger today." The chorus reiterates the reasonableness of his idea, even though a contrary opinion is expressed in a sign stating, "No credit—especially you, Wimpy!" The pacing is perfect; each shot is carefully selected and timed to reveal the simultaneous events occurring in the café, and the viewer perceives that there is a great deal happening beyond the frame. The song ends as Popeye gives Wimpy his hamburger and tells him why he is looking for his father. His monologue is interrupted by the rude laughter and insults of the Roughhouse gang. When the gang insults his father and molests several townspeople, particularly Ham Gravy (Bill Irwin), who is forced to offer "my most humfelt and sincere apologies," Popeye finds that his "sensk of humilgration" has been offended. He quickly teaches the gang members some manners. No one is seriously hurt in the fight, not even Butch, whose head is used as a punching bag by Popeye. Everyone learns that from now on, good will win over bad, and that the new winner in town is the stranger with the huge forearms.

From these sequences alone one recognizes the great achievement of Robin Williams in bringing the very difficult character of Popeye to life. First, a tremendous vocal range is evident. The inflections range from a smooth, melodious tone used in conversations, for example, with the Oyls, to the grating tone that seems to sneak into his voice at times. His voice achieves gutteral perfection when he adds "believe it or not" onto the end of "Blow Me Down," or in his last "I yam wot I yam" from that scene. There is a slightly different inflection and speed of delivery for each emotional or ideological nuance. When he sings "I Yam Wot I Yam," for instance, Williams uses volume, pitch, and pace changes to declare and emphasize his identity to everyone at the racetrack on Derbyday. Aware of the presence of "venerable disease" in this seedy area of town, he begins to sing that he will have to "gird up my loins for this one." Not even Bluto can argue with him when he repeats, quickly and emphatically, "I yam wot I yam, I'm Popeye da Sailor Man."

To understand why this is an important declaration, and not solipsism, one must remember that Sweethaven is a bastion of conformity. Popeye's proclamation of individuality is accepted without question, just as the decrees of Bluto, speaking for the invisible Commodore (Ray Walston), and the judgments of the Taxman are accepted without debate. By declaring he is not a part of their society, Popeye immediately secures a position of authority in that culture. So the people of Sweethaven rally around Popeye in his fights against Oxblood Oxheart (Peter Bray), the Taxman, and Bluto, and in his struggle to recover his adopted child. "I yam wot I yam," then, is not, as it is often argued, a redundant or meaningless ideological claim. It is in fact an active declaration of war against a life-style that is "safe from democracy" and against oppression and fear.

Characterization

Although the narrative of the film is minimal, it does emphasize the notion of Popeye as a nonconformist whose activities significantly improve and unify a chaotic society. First Popeye comes between Bluto and Olive, and then he develops a relationship with her that is strengthened with the discovery and adoption of another outsider, Swee' Pea. After Bluto spots the precognizant abilities of Swee' Pea at the racetrack, he kidnaps the child, an action that the viewer knows will force a confrontation between Bluto and Popeye. While tracking down Bluto, Popeye discovers his father—"same bulgy arms, same squinky eye"—and the Commodore is glad to join him in the quest. The townspeople are not just curious bystanders anymore; they follow Popeye to Scab Island, where Bluto, with the help of Swee' Pea, is searching for buried treasure. Popeye and friends rescue Swee' Pea, he saves Olive from the octopus, and he chases Bluto out to sea forever. The crowd applauds and sings, because they know that their lives will be simpler and happier now, with Popeye as their invincible protector. They will continue to chase their hats, gamble on Derbyday, or sing about food, but they no longer will shake in their boots or faint out of their clothes at the mention of the name of Bluto, the Commodore, or for that matter, Popeye.

Each of the main figures in *Popeye* is a perfect foil for the hero. For example, Wimpy is bold and naive enough to kidnap Swee' Pea twice— betraying Popeye the second time for a bag of thirty hamburgers. Olive

Oyl undergoes several personality changes. When she first meets Popeye, she has "a good mind to have my father call a policeman," and she wonders, "What kind of name is that? Popeye? Pretty strange!" But after the discovery of Swee' Pea, her demeanor changes. She is more pleasant in general, and much more affectionate toward Popeye. When she banters, "I said phooey and I mean phooey! Phooey!" it is an obvious admission of her love. Their warm relationship continues until her attitudes again change, this time at Derbyday, when she sides with Wimpy against Popeye. His position about the racetrack gambling is unshakable. He declares, "Me chilt will not be exploitikated fer ill-gotten games." Olive sees the 120 semolians that Swee' Pea has won by predicting the race winners and screams, "It's not ill-gotten, it's good-gotten! These gains will feed us and clothe us and save us!" So the battle lines are drawn and explicit: Olive wants to use Swee' Pea to get rich, while Popeye refuses to accede to the allure of pragmatism. When he takes Swee' Pea from her, he declares that "moraliky ain't doughnuts," and so "a fodder gotta duty ta pertek his orphink from chilt abusk." The couple is reconciled only when Olive risks everything to help him rescue the child. Through Olive the viewer learns the exact nature of Popeye's commitment to Swee' Pea and the extent of his rejection of the relative morality that Olive and the people of Sweethaven possess.

Reception

While Robert Altman was still shooting the film, Robert Evans began publicizing it. In May 1980, after a visit to Malta, Evans began screening clips and songs from *Popeye* before audiences of children, teenagers, and the press in the United States. He wanted to determine if young audiences would be as elated and enthusiastic as he was over this "celebration of the individual." While he avoided Malta most of the time, he had to quell the fears of Paramount about going over budget and soothe the occasional flare-ups of tempers between his screenwriter and the cast. Despite these diplomatic exigencies, and the complication of constructing a tank in an undersea cave for the octopus fight, the principal photography was completed on schedule on 1 July 1980. The editing took two months in Malta and at Lion's Gate. Notwithstanding his claims, Robert Evans had little to do with the editing. He was busy spending another $2 million on a publicity blitz.

The film was held for a Christmas release and was premiered on 6 December at Mann's Chinese Theater, with proceeds going to the Los Angeles Children's Museum. The film opened in Los Angeles on 9 December and nationwide three days later. *Popeye* was a box-office success. It earned $6 million in the first three days of release, $32 million in

thirty-two days, and $44 million after three months, when it was republi-
cized and rereleased.

Needless to say, Robert Altman was elated about everything concerning
Popeye—except for the critical response to the film. None of the critics
really enjoyed the film. Vincent Canby in the *New York Times* (12 December), David Denby in *New York* (29 December), and Pauline Kael in the
New Yorker (5 January) all complained that the film was generally too detached. Canby called it "tentative and restrained," "not boisterous." Kael
felt the film was "too distant," that Altman was "trying too hard." Denby
called it a "private picture," a film with a style that made it so inaccessible
that the viewer could not become emotionally involved "with people who
aren't people." On the West Coast, *Variety* (10 December) declared that
the film "failed to bring the characters to life" and that it was only in the
last hour, when the characters "fall back on their cartoon craziness that the
picture works at all." Most critics commented that if Altman had worked
with a more experienced screenwriter the results would have been better.
Andrew Sarris alone pointed out in his *Village Voice* article (17 December)
that the "stylized gestures and movement inherent in the very idea of a
live action *Popeye*" were well represented in the Altman film.

For the most part, these negative commentaries are difficult to dispute
because the reactions are very personal and closely tied to perceptions of
Popeye and of Altman films. There were certainly no ground rules, no
general aesthetic standards for how a live-action cartoon should engage its
viewers. Even if such a systematic approach had been outlined, it would
be inappropriate to think that *Popeye* should be judged solely on that basis. The only fruitful way to analyze *Popeye* is to point out some general
areas of interest, and then to indicate the latitude of interpretations, emotions, and concerns that could be reasonably generated by the average
viewer.

Considering its intended audience, one needs to determine if the film
is entertaining. Watching a live cartoon character for two hours could be a
trying experience for anyone. In pacing the second half of the film, Altman
intuitively stressed action and not dialogue, so there are fights, a long
chase scene, and underwater struggles. If Altman had not taken such care
in presenting the characters in the first half of the film, however, the response to the second half would be apathy. Of course, the first half of the
film also contains delightful antics, songs, and ample anecdotes to enter-
tain all but the most detached viewers.

Second, one should consider whether or not the world of *Popeye* is just
too confusing and too chaotic to be appreciated. The action is frenetic,
periodically. But *Popeye* is structured around the title character; he is in
nearly every scene in the film. If one is not comfortable with that character, one would be tempted to conclude that the structure is poor.

Altman wanted to keep his characters "silhouettes." The wisdom of that decision could be debated, but the overriding concern must be whether or not Popeye is a captivating character. He is trustworthy, honest, hard-working, and individualistic, but is he boring? The character could have been done differently. But does Robert Altman's Popeye stimulate a degree of delight, apprehension, curiosity, sympathy, and interest in the viewer? If so, then the "one-dimensionality" and "stylization" debates are largely academic.

A third, reasonable concern about *Popeye* is that of the quality of the music and humor in the film. As in *Nashville*, some songs in *Popeye* are simply better than others. "He's Large" is probably the worst, with "It's Not Easy Being Me" a close second. The melodies, lyrics, and performances of those two pieces are definitely poor. On the other hand, one cannot imagine a more fitting, ambiguous, or pleasant anthem than "Sweethaven." "Blow Me Down," with its easygoing philosophy and unobtrusive dance steps, is a good companion piece for "I Yam Wot I Yam;" its force, delivery, and argument are intimidating. Similarly, not all the jokes or peripheral activity in *Popeye* make sense, but the list of inspired, amusing movements, gestures, and jokes is endless. It would be unfair to judge the film adversely because some of the gags do not work well. One could balance off the first Popeye/Bluto fight, which is not very interesting, with the wonderfully choreographed fighting in the Roughhouse Café. That form of criticism would be too subjective, however, to be of any value to the viewer. It is probably more helpful to point out that the shots are fast enough and the scream long-enough delayed to make the quick scene of the Mailman (David Arkin) putting his hand on the steam pipe very funny. On the other hand, the orders and movements of the commodore on the bridge are too uncontrolled and too repetitious to be amusing to most people.

There are also some very valid grounds for criticizing *Popeye*. Too much attention is paid to Swee' Pea. The child is supposed to represent hope for the future, but he is on screen too frequently. A second problem is a lack of substantive characterizations in the screenplay—which resulted from the disagreements between Feiffer and Altman throughout the film. It was largely Robert Altman's role to fill in the script with his own imaginative, peripheral characters from the comic strip, such as Mrs. Oxheart, Bill Barnacle, and Ham Gravy. Often these characters have nothing to say. In fact, the final draft of the screenplay was completely redone in the shooting. This was of course not new for Altman, but it was the first time his screenwriter took exception to the changes to this degree. Usually Altman and his screenwriter (Joan Tewkesbury, for example) would work cooperatively on changes during the shooting. Feiffer and Altman never could.

Finally, the weakest part of the film is the final twenty minutes, which is nothing more than a long and not very interesting chase scene and fist fight. This "cartoon craziness" is in fact present throughout the film, but at the end Popeye runs out of dialogue and all Olive can do is scream for help. What is conspicuously lacking here is Popeye's amused, cynical mutterings and arguments, for it is his vibrant sarcasm that keeps the film alive and moving in several otherwise slow moments. Robert Altman would be the first person to admit that his films have a polarizing effect. Half his audience loves his work, while the other half cannot get involved in what he creates. *Popeye* has that same effect on its viewers. With *Popeye*, a great number of people were sufficiently interested to see the film many times, in spite of the negative criticism that surrounded the film upon its release. *Popeye* received as much widespread attention and recognition as *M*A*S*H* or *Nashville,* and it was with this unpredictable, challenging project that the director once again came to the forefront of American cinema.

The Breakup of Lion's Gate

Before the release of *Popeye,* Robert Altman began working on a film called *Lone Star,* written by Will Trisher, with Sigourney Weaver and Powers Boothe. But after at least four months of preparation, United Artists head H. Averbach told the press that it was going to be canceled because of a problem with Altman, specifically, his delay in the starting date for shooting. Altman maintained that the studio was simply scared of a possible financial loss, and dropped it without warning after he had spent half a year on preproduction development.

This was the last straw for Altman. He began dissolving his interests and commitments to Lion's Gate, and soon the studio was sold in its entirety for $2.3 million. He began directing one-act plays at the Los Angeles Actor's Theater. In November 1981 he took two of the plays by Frank South, *Precious Blood* and *Rattlesnake in the Cooler,* to the St. Clements Theater, Off-Broadway, where they had a successful run. It was at this time that he announced that he was through with commercial filmmaking, for the same reasons that he had opposed studio and conglomerate Hollywood control throughout his career. He picked up options on two plays, *The Hold-Up* by Marsha Norman and *The Diviners* by Jim Leonard. He let both options stand for a while, and decided to try his hand at opera. He directed *The Rake's Progress* in Ann Arbor. Meanwhile he negotiated to direct a play on Broadway entitled *Come Back to the Five and Dime, Jimmy Dean, Jimmy Dean,* and it was to film this play that Altman ended his sabbatical from cinema.

11

Come Back to the Five and Dime, Jimmy Dean, Jimmy Dean

THE WORLDWIDE RELEASE OF *Come Back to the Five and Dime, Jimmy Dean, Jimmy Dean* in 1982 revealed, once again, a glaring discrepancy between critical response and audience reception to Altman films. When a ten-minute standing ovation ended the United States premiere of *Jimmy Dean* at the Chicago Film Festival, 30 September 1982, Altman joked, "Why don't we quit while we're ahead?" In the following question-and-answer session with the audience, and in a brief interview later that evening, Altman explained the plans, intentions, and techniques at work in *Come Back to the Five and Dime, Jimmy Dean, Jimmy Dean.*

The inspiration for the film came of course from the Ed Graczyk drama, which Altman directed on Broadway, where it ran for sixty performances before closing, at the author's request. Altman then received approximately $800,000 from Showtime Video/Viacom, through Mark Goodson Productions, to film the play. He maintained that he originally planned *Jimmy Dean* as a theatrical film, and that "the initial press report that it was made for cable is not true." He shot the film in "dead sequence," using a "redressed set" from the stage play. *Jimmy Dean* was filmed in super 16mm, using "full 35mm negatives for the first answer print," and for the required multiple prints. "I don't think we could have done any better in 35mm—so there was no need for it." He did the editing in collaboration with Jason Rosenfield. Then Altman refused to release the film through a major studio because he was "not going to let the film be thrown away" as *Health* was. He used a small New York company called Cinecom International Films to open *Jimmy Dean* in the United States "on the art film circuit," in order "to guarantee a long play."

Altman spoke at length at the Chicago premiere about the casting and set design of the film: "I didn't do what they told me I had to do, I hired the people I wanted," a statement that accurately reflects his approach to filmmaking for the past thirty years. Specifically, he recalled, "When we were casting the play, we called Shelley Duvall—she had just done *Pop-*

A last reunion in Jimmy Dean: top, *Joanne (Karen Black) and Sissy (Cher) with Juanita (Sudie Bond). Courtesy of John Iltis Associates, Chicago, IL;* bottom, *Mona (Sandy Dennis) joins Joanne and Sissy in an Andrews Sisters singalong. Courtesy of John Iltis Associates, Chicago, IL.*

eye," but he felt that "the balance wasn't correct" this time with Duvall. So while he was casting the other roles and talking to Duvall, he learned that Cher was in New York. He called her, but had "no positive opinion about her." He told her, "If you're really serious, read for it." After seeing her on stage, he encouraged her and "believed in her." Thus Cher made her acting debut as the smart-mouthed, buxom waitress Sissy in *Come Back to the Five and Dime.*

Altman felt that the demands on the director moving from stage to screen were easy, while "the actors had the most adjustments to make. I just slid into it." Altman felt that Karen Black's performance "on film was considerably different than on stage," and that the audience should feel "more empathy for her on film" than on stage. Overall, the director felt that the transition "opened up the play": in rehearsals "the actresses were so good it amazed me"; and on film the play seemed less "external." Still, he wanted to create a "claustrophobic feeling," while "not having the audience bored" by this "nerve-wracking experience." Thus the task was more complicated for Altman than he admitted.

Controversial Techniques

The main device Altman employed in filming the play captured a great amount of critical attention. Altman constructed a double set, with two-way mirrors, through which he could move from the present to the past. All that was required to change time was to "dissolve through the mirrors" with the help of some "computerized theatrical lighting." Thus in the film the audience sees two interior sets of the five and dime store, one next to the other, one the mirror image of the other. He confined the present actions to one side, the past to the other, with the mirror dividing the sets.

The technique apparently caused more problems for most critics than it did for Altman. They contended that the "flashy" and "gimmicky" device upset narrative and thematic continuity. Pauline Kael did concede that the film "shouldn't work, but it does." Responding to critics' reviews in a *Boston Globe* interview (14 January 1983) Altman said, "The critical reaction doesn't surprise me. Nothing surprises me any more. I take that back. One thing surprised me when I showed *Jimmy Dean* at film festivals—no one walked out."

Similar criticisms are made of the time-frame at the end of the film, which the director, in his typically quixotic manner, described as occurring "maybe 20 years later—or that's the way it always was." Neither that comment nor his remark that "the ending is an emotional response that occurred to us" is purposefully oblique; it is consistent with his stance on interpretations of his films: "I feel as an artist, I can draw things out to you as I see it, and you bring something of yourself to the film." He denied that he is always being negative in his films, answering that "this is my culture, my heritage that I love. Maybe we are just a little too close."

Before the Chicago premiere, Altman screened *Jimmy Dean* at film festivals in Montreal, Toronto, Belgium, Venice, Deauville, and Paris, and was "amazed at its reception" and by the numerous prizes it won. He had guessed that audience response might be as high as 60–40 for the film, and the film response far exceeded his expectations in each of those cities. He told his Chicago audience, "I never have had a film of mine received as well as this film—I don't understand it, but I like it!" In Chicago the film won the festival's grand prize. *Jimmy Dean* opened a week later in New York, Los Angeles, Chicago, and other primary art-film markets, where it played for nearly two months to fairly successful gates.

Story Line

Come Back to the Five and Dime, Jimmy Dean, Jimmy Dean is essentially a simple story of the twentieth reunion of six members of a Jimmy Dean fan club at a dimestore in McCarthy, Texas. The members are Jo (Karen Black), Stella Mae (Kathy Bates), Edna Louise (Marta Heflin), Mona (Sandy Dennis), and Sissy (Cher). Juanita (Sudie Bond) is the store proprietor. Through a series of conversations, jokes, and arguments, occurring in the present and in flashbacks, each of the women reveals, discovers, and refutes secrets she has held for twenty years.

The action opens inside the five and dime in the present with a radio playing in the background. It is raining, and the waitress Sissy wanders by while Juanita offers refreshments to Mona and Edna Louise, who still live in the town. Altman dissolves to a flasback as Mona questions "why that fatal crash took his life away." We see a neon-lit picture of Jimmy Dean and Jesus, a mirror, and light bulb. Another dissolve returns the viewer to the present, as Mona states, "I'm sure they'll all remember what it was like here—in the five and dime" at the time of the shooting of the George Stevens film *Giant*, the event that brought James Dean to Texas in the 1950s. In a series of quick dissolves from present to past, the women, particularly Mona, preach about the memory of James Dean; they talk about old friends, including Joe and Lester T., and we learn that Mona has apparently had a son by James Dean. Stella Mae arrives, and we hear fragments of conversation: "it is real—it's just deceiving to the eye"; "it's the heat—plays tricks with your emotions if you're not careful"; and "but he lives on in his movies." Mona mentions again that she was an extra in a scene in *Giant*, and we hear "that boy certainly was a boon to us—made our Woolworth's the busiest five and dime in all Texas."

After several other flashbacks and conversations, Karen Black enters, tells everyone her name is Jo, for Joanne, and remarks how it appears that "the McGuire sisters are reunited." Each of the women feels that there is something familiar about Jo. At this point she reveals that she was Joe, the only man in the fan club, before leaving town and undergoing a sex-change operation. She receives the amazed and disgusted responses of her friends. Meanwhile Stella Mae, whose prurient nature has been stimulated by this topic, presses Jo to learn the technical and biological details of her transformation.

After several flashbacks in which we see the girls joking, singing, and arguing, their conversations in the present become increasingly acerbic. Several of the women discuss exactly how dumb they think Edna Louise is, and they agree that nothing in life is ever simple. Mona then begins her lengthy monologue and describes how, during the shooting of *Giant*, she was an extra; and how, in one scene, she was visible, "peeking out from behind the left ear" of Elizabeth Taylor. Mona says that James Dean had spotted her there, approached her, and slept with her, which resulted in her son, Jimmy Dean. During her speech, Altman cuts to the picture of James Dean and of Joe's face, superimposing it over Joanne's face in the mirror.

After she tells her story, Jo shocks all the women by telling how there really was no meeting with James Dean and certainly no son by James Dean. She reminds Mona that, as Joe, "he" had loved her and slept with her, and that young Jimmy Dean was their son. In a flashback we see Joe yelling at Mona, "Just because he is dead, don't you kill me off, too!"

The silence is broken and the women begin revealing other truths. The pace of these catharses quickens. Joe was in love with Mona. Lester T., who was Sissy's boyfriend, had sodomized Joe. After her operation, Jo met Lester T. in Kansas City. He did not recognize her, and through him Jo learned tht Sissy had undergone radical mastectomies. Sissy then recounts her traumatic experience, explaining why she resisted the operation and the importance of her physical appearance to Lester T. She is forced to admit that Lester T. has abandoned her and is not on a business trip as she previously informed everyone. Next, everyone in the group begins to deride Edna Louise; only Jo is happy about the pregnancy and tells Edna Louise that she "glows." Jo believes that Stella Mae is jealous of Edna Louise. Stella Mae laughs, but when pressured she shouts, "I'm happy, goddam it!" The film ends with another double-set shot of the interiors while, ironically, the song "Sincerely" plays in the background. The credits roll over shots of the deserted five and dime, a hauntingly brilliant conclusion since there will obviously be no "next meeting in twenty years." The image of the abandoned five and dime slowly fading out adds an other-worldliness to all the events that occurred at the reunion. Clearly the "present" in the play is not the present in real time. This device makes the actions that occurred within and outside the five and dime appear less stagey and more as though they are really happening, but in a nonspecific time and space.

Problems for the Audience

Watching *Jimmy Dean* is a more demanding experience than viewing any other recent Altman film. Except for the occasions when Cher mimics the nervous mannerisms of Sandy Dennis and the jokes of Stella Mae, there is little humor in the film. Nothing relieves the drama and the tragedy of the lives of these women. Unlike *Buffalo Bill, Quintet, A Perfect Couple, A Wedding,* or *Popeye,* there are no characters in *Jimmy Dean* that are immediately likable. The audience identifies more closely with Jo than with any of the other women, but the nervousness that is infused in each of her phrases and actions forces the viewer to mistrust her. The other women do not seem to like each other. After twenty years all they manage to do is fight, argue, and cry. These disagreeable interactions warn the viewer to be cautious extending sympathy to any of the women. The overwhelming viewer response to the group is pity, not sympathy or friendship.

The reasons for the limited appeal of the characters are quite complex. Most of the women's problems are physical or sexual ones. Stella Mae's husband cannot have children; Edna Louise cannot stop from having them. Sissy has undergone a mastectomy; Jo is a transsexual. The father of Mona's child is a woman. One glance at Juanita tells the viewer that she is terminally ill. The characters in *A Wedding* of course have similar problems (e.g., Buffy Brenner's promiscuity), but in that film, the events are not as unrelentingly depressing. The admissions in *A Wedding* are nicely spaced; the problems are not exclusively physical; and the sets are varied and appropriate to the present lives of the characters. Also, *A Wedding* is easier to follow because the viewer is let in on many secrets before they become common knowledge to the characters. This process is reversed in *Jimmy Dean,* which makes identification with the characters more tentative.

Altman deals with the problems of the characters in *Jimmy Dean* in a deadly serious manner. The women's conversations seem unrelenting, and an atmosphere of tension and insecurity pervades. The women here are perfect tools for Altman. He carefully establishes the way Americans manage pretensions and lies in their lives. Given the limitations of viewer identification with the characters in the film, his style is surprisingly convincing. In a way, these pained people are more disturbing than are the members of the families in *A Wedding,* the politicians in *Nashville,* or Charlie and Bill in *California Split* because they have flaws we can see in ourselves. Their goals and actions are fairly obtuse, but the problems are not as alien as they may seem at first. The notion of a twentieth reunion of a James Dean fan club seems grotesque. The secrets that are divulged seem petty and contrived. The locale seems too rural and stagey. The scandals appear to be seamy and voyeuristic. These people look peculiar doing these things on the screen, and this is the basic and very scary perception Altman is communicating—that when people adopt pretensions and live in self-serving fantasies, their lives are indeed petty, tawdry, and contrived. So *Jimmy Dean* is difficult to watch because it is the story of people existing in an emotional vacuum, slowly living through each other's gradual, imperceptible death.

These women are so emotionally drained by secrets and lies that even frank, blunt accusations that would be anathema in society do not affect them any more. Mona has been made aware, for example, of a serious flaw in her character. She could change her life, but she prefers to maintain the pretense because of jealousy and pride. She chooses to believe that she can joke her way through any problem in life.

Altman has delineated a set of social and psychological forces in this film more subtle than the events that drove Cathryn *(Images)* to murder, and of a greater magnitude than the lies that pushed Buffalo Bill into a hallucinatory retreat. The emotional drama in *Jimmy Dean* is painful to watch because Altman forces the audience to wonder how much human sensitivity has been lost in life. The process of denial that we witness here is, as Altman suspected, uncomfortably close to our lives.

Many critics argued that the "deep dark secrets" in *Jimmy Dean* were not very deep. This charge misses a central issue of the film. The secrets in *Jimmy Dean* are dramatic devices through which Altman can lead us into the characters and can suggest some reasons for their interactions. Altman could not have directed sixty performances of *Jimmy Dean* on stage without having devised detailed plans for drawing the viewer into the interior realm of each character. If one looks beyond the surface revelations, past the unattractiveness of the characters, then one may notice that the boredom and bickering experienced by these people are both common and disturbing. This is an involved and risky technique of characterization, but it works.

The emotional turmoil of *Jimmy Dean* begs for a comparison to *Images*. Although similar ideas are involved in both films—an inner reality that conflicts with an objective reality—the answer that Altman invents for Cathryn is blatant and harsh, while the resolution in *Jimmy Dean* is ambiguous. Cathryn's motivations are obtuse and obscure. The rationale for the women's behaviors becomes transparent in *Jimmy Dean*. Cathryn indulges herself in fantasies; Joanne forces each woman to see the truth about herself. Ultimately, *Images* is a psychological exposé, while *Jimmy Dean* is a social and cultural mural.

Come Back to the Five and Dime, Jimmy Dean, Jimmy Dean has many performances that make it interesting to study. It is apparent in this film that, unfortunately, Marta Heflin cannot act, and her presence makes the film sluggish at times. She is too stiff, too much of a pathetic, cardboard figure. Edna Louise is not a simple role, but, as in *A Perfect Couple*, Heflin seems to be out of touch with her character and with the others in the film. She probably would have been more effective in each film in a smaller and simpler role. While Sandy Dennis, the other Altman veteran, quivers and bites her lip a lot, she is nonetheless convincing in the role of a woman who has lived with a fantasy for so long that it has drastically affected her life. In some ways her role is a reprise of Frances Austen from *That Cold Day in the Park*. Finally, it is easy to see Altman's style in the characterizations of Stella Mae and Joanne. Stella Mae is an exciting and talkative character. Altman withholds the secret about her "problem" until the very end of the film, thus increasing the viewer's curiosity and causing the viewer to withhold any negative judgments. When the aesthetic, androgynous Jo and the pregnant Edna Louise finally defuse her character, bringing Stella Mae's "femininity" into question, the viewer realizes that this extroverted member of the club is just as superficial as the others.

Altman manages to keep tight control over his characters in *Jimmy Dean*, moving them from carefully planned stage performances to the screen, using more traditionally theatrical rehearsals than in any previous film. As a result, *Jimmy Dean* may be another instance of an Altman paradox: the more controls and limitations that are placed on him, the more finely crafted, intricate, and tight his work is.

It is fascinating that, after *The James Dean Story*, Altman would select another project touching upon the life of James Dean. Dean was born in film and sustained in the media. Like Buffalo Bill, he has now become a myth—he is magic. The women in *Jimmy Dean* are trying to escape reality by associating themselves with this magic, this fantasy, even if it is just for a moment. They cannot escape the limits of their culture through Dean, however, because he is in fact a creation of that culture.

The reference to the James Dean myth is a clue to Altman's pervasive film message. Altman knows that James Dean had the kind of screen presence and magic that caused people to "give in" to cinema. Altman is often able to imbue his characters with that charisma, those special qualities that stimulate the viewer to the same level of enthusiasm and rapport that James Dean commanded. In each film Altman strives to reinforce and respond to that essential need—to give in to cinema. By reiterating that experience in his films, Robert Altman helps his audiences learn something more about themselves and their culture.

Streamers

Streamers is the second of the films based on plays that Altman has produced and directed since his "retirement" from cinema. First presented on stage in New Haven, the David Rabe play was then produced Off-Broadway by Joseph Papp and directed by Mike Nichols.

The action and discussions in Altman's film occur on one set, and a slowly building sense of imprisonment in the viewer corresponds to the attitudes of the characters, who have been inducted into the army to serve in Vietnam. The production was additionally demanding for cast and crew since all the action occurs only in the last fifteen minutes, preceded by very tense, emotional revelations of the characters' sexual identities and their attitudes toward war and life. In an interview in November 1983, Mitchell Lichenstein (Richie) described how helpful Altman was in imparting to the cast and crew a sense of cooperation and continuity while shooting *Streamers*.

The film is as bewildering and shocking as *Images.* But in *Streamers* the discussions are more poignant, the symbolism much more specific, and the deaths so tragic that ultimately the viewer wishes that these encounters were only hallucinations, as in *Images,* and indeed not horribly real manifestations of violence.

Notes and References

Chapter One

1. Judith Kass, *Robert Altman: American Innovator* (New York, 1978), p. 9.
2. Cinema Arts Directors Series Interviews, no. 13152 (New York, 1978), side 1 (cassette-recorded).
3. Todd McCarthy and Charles Flynn, *Kings of the Bs* (New York, 1975), p. 216.
4. Charles Michener, "Action Director," *Newsweek*, 11 March 1974, p. 88.
5. Robert Altman, speaking on "The Dick Cavett Show," PBS, October 1978.
6. Mary Murphy, "Crisis of a Cult Figure," *New West*, 23 May 1977, p. 36.

Chapter Two

1. James Monaco, *American Film Now* (New York, 1979), p. 319.
2. Bob Thomas, ed., *Directors in Action* (Indianapolis: Bobbs Merrill, 1973), p. 61.
3. William Froug, *The Screenwriter Looks at the Screenwriter* (New York, 1972), p. 128.
4. Jan Dawson, "*M*A*S*H*," *Sight and Sound*, Summer 1970, p. 161.
5. William Johnson, "*M*A*S*H*," *Film Quarterly* 23 no. 3 (Spring 1970):38.
6. Pauline Kael, *Deeper Into Movies* (Boston: Little, Brown, 1970), p. 92.
7. Richard Corliss, *Talking Pictures* (New York: Overlook Press, 1974), p. 342.

Chapter Three

1. Bruce Williamson, "Robert Altman," interview, *Playboy*, August 1976, p. 160.

2.   Cannon had previously written *Skidoo* for Otto Preminger; his *Brewster* treatment reached Altman through Ingo Preminger.

3.   *On Making A Movie: Brewster McCloud* (New York, 1971).

4.   David Johnson, "Robert Altman," *Show*, October 1972, p. 49.

5.   Roberta Rubenstein, *"Brewster McCloud," Film Quarterly* 25, no. 2 (Winter 1971–72):44.

6.   Michael Dempsey, "Altman: The Empty Staircase and the Chinese Princess," *Film Comment* 10 (September–October 1974):10.

7.   Kael, *Deeper Into Movies*, p. 280.

Chapter Four

1.   Robert Altman, Papers for *McCabe and Mrs. Miller*, University of Wisconsin State Archives (Madison, Wisconsin), box 1, folder 8.

2.   Jacoba Atlas and Ann Guerin, "Robert Altman, Julie Christie, and Warren Beatty Make the Western Real," *Show*, August 1971, p. 18.

3.   Robert Altman Papers, box 1, folder 12.

4.   Aljean Harmetz, "The 15th Man Who Was Asked to Direct *M*A*S*H* (And Did) Makes a Peculiar Western," *New York Times Magazine*, 20 June 1971, p. 52.

5.   Arthur Knight, "The Technics and Techniques of Film," *Saturday Review*, August 1971, p. 50.

6.   Jan Dawson, *"McCabe and Mrs. Miller," Sight and Sound*, Autumn 1971), p. 221.

7.   Jackson Burgess, *"McCabe and Mrs. Miller," Film Quarterly* 25, no. 2 (Winter 1971–72):52.

8.   Pauline Kael, *"McCabe and Mrs. Miller," New Yorker*, 3 July 1971, p. 80.

Chapter Five

1.   Robert Altman, *Images* (Los Angeles, 1966), p. 45.

2.   Vincent Canby, "'Runaway Robert' Altman," *New York Times*, 15 December 1972, sec. 2, p. 4.

3.   See Columbia Pictures' "Publicity File" for *Images* (1972).

4.   Julian C. Rice, "Transcendental Pornography and *Taxi Driver*," *Journal of Popular Film* 5, no. 2 (1976):113.

5.   Bruce Cook, "Bob and Pauline: A Fickle Affair," *American Film*, December–January 1978), p. 7.

6.   Richard Combs, *"Images," Sight and Sound*, Winter 1971–72, p. 51.

Chapter Six

1.   Jan Dawson, "Robert Altman Speaking," *Film Comment*, March–April 1974, p. 41.

2. Charles Gregory, "Knight Without Meaning," *Sight and Sound*, Summer 1973, p. 156.

3. Pauline Kael, "Movieland—The Bums' Paradise," *New Yorker*, 22 October 1973, p. 149.

4. James Powers, ed., "Dialogue on Film: Joan Tewkesbury," *American Film* 4, no. 3 (March 1979):45.

5. Pauline Kael, "Love and Coca-Cola," *New Yorker*, 30 January 1974, p. 92.

6. Marsha Kinder, "Return of the Outlaw Couple," *Film Quarterly* 27, no. 4 (Summer 1974):2–10.

Chapter Seven

1. Terry Curtis Fox, "*Nashville* Chats," *Chicago Reader*, 4 July 1975, p. 2.

2. Janet Maslin, "Michael Murphy, Actor, Plays 'Guys You Love to Hate,'" *New York Times*, 11 June 1978, sec. 1, p. 61.

3. Charles Michener and Martin Kasindorf, "Altman's Opryland Epic," *Newsweek*, 30 June 1975, p. 50.

4. Paramount Pictures, *Press Book: Nashville* (New York: *Paramount Pictures*, 1975), p. 2.

5. Connie Byrne and William Lopez, "*Nashville*," *Film Quarterly* 29, no. 2 (Winter 1975–76):19.

6. Hollis Alpert, "The Homecoming of Barbara Jean," *Saturday Review*, 28 June 1975, p. 40.

7. Kael desired to "break" the *Nashville* story, and she wanted those first words to be favorable. For her early review she was immediately attacked by Vincent Canby, Penelope Gilliat, and Andrew Sarris. Previously Kael had reviewed *Thieves Like Us* twelve days before its premiere.

8. John Simon, "The Amazing Shrunken *Nashville*," *Esquire*, September 1975, p. 34.

Chapter Eight

1. Michael Billington, "Arthur Kopit Talks About *Wings*," *New York Times*, 25 June 1975, sec. 2, p. 6.

2. Jay Monaghan, *The Great Rascal* (Boston, 1951).

3. Charles Higham, "How *Ragtime* Led to Discord," *New York Times*, 20 September 1976, sec. 2, p. 15.

4. Noe Goldwasser, "Altman Refuses Berlin Award," *Village Voice*, 26 July 1976, p. 102.

5. Andrew Sarris, "Bottom Line Buffalos Altman," *Village Voice*, 5 July 1976, p. 108.

6. Joan Mellen, "Hollywood Rediscovers the American Woman," *New York Times*, 23 April 1978, sec. 2, p. 15.

7. Annick Geille, "Robert Altman and Women," *Playboy,* French edition, August 1977, p. 17.

Chapter Nine

1. Speaking on "The Dick Cavett Show," PBS, September 1978.
2. Mary Murphy, "Crisis of a Cult Figure," *New West,* 23 May 1977), p. 43.
3. Lauren Hutton, speaking on "Dinah," 28 April 1978.
4. Speaking in a personal interview, Chicago, Illinois, 11 January 1978.
5. Roger Ebert, "Best Man: Altman Plans to Have Fun Giving Away the Bride," *Chicago Sun-Times,* 12 June 1977, sec. 3, p. 1.
6. Gene Siskel, "*Wedding* Is Set, but Honeymoon Is Delayed," *Chicago Tribune,* 16 April 1978, sec. 6, p. 2.
7. Speaking in a personal interview at the premiere of *A Wedding,* Chicago, Illinois, 28 April 1978.
8. Andrew Sarris, "New Pillars of the Pantheon," *Village Voice,* 3 July 1978, p. 40.
9. Charles Michener, "Robert Altman Interview," *Film Comment,* September-October 1978, p. 17.
10. Vincent Canby, "Altman—A Daring Filmmaker Falters," *New York Times,* 18 February 1979, sec. 2, p. 1.
11. Michener, "Robert Altman Interview," p. 18.
12. Judy Stone, "'If a Director Tells Me, I Follow Him,'" *New York Times,* 4 February 1979, sec. 2, p. 17.
13. "Robert Altman Company Sets up Plant for Self and Tenants," *Variety,* 7 February 1979, p. 49. (See also "Robert Altman Expands Lion's Gate Films," *Millimeter,* April 1979, p. 122.)

Chapter Ten

1. Jennifer Allen, "*Popeye,*" *Life,* 6 October 1980, p. 91.
2. "The Stormy Saga of *Popeye,*" *American Film,* December 1980, p. 36.

Selected Bibliography

1. Books

Altman, Robert, and **Rudolph, Alan.** *Buffalo Bill and the Indians, Or, Sitting Bull's History Lesson.* New York: Bantam Books, 1976. The original screen story and screenplay, along with a synopsis "told" to Altman and Rudolph by the Hon. William F. Cody. Contains stills of all the Wild West players.

Karp, Alan. *The Films of Robert Altman.* Metuchen, N.J.: Scarecrow Press, 1981. A loosely organized study of Altman's films divided into the categories of "themes and structures," "genre and myths," and "films and dreams." No filmography.

Kass, Judith M. *Robert Altman: American Innovator.* New York: Popular Library, 1978. A recounting of plots and themes in Altman films to *Three Women.* No notes or bibliography.

McClelland, C. Kirk. *On Making a Movie: Brewster McCloud.* New York: New American Library, 1971. A daily production journal, with cast sketches, the shooting script, and the original Cannon screenplay. No index or bibliography.

Tewkesbury, Joan. *Nashville.* New York: Bantam Books, 1976. The original screenplay, with a preface by Tewkesbury on politics and the film. Complete with stills, credits, song lyrics, and the Walker platform (parts of which became the Walker public address announcements).

2. Parts of books

AuWerter, Russell. "Robert Altman." In *Directors in Action.* Edited by Bob Thomas. New York: Bobbs Merrill, 1973, pp. 60–65. A detailed interview with Altman on the making of *M*A*S*H* and *Brewster McCloud.*

Dick, Bernard. *"Nashville."* In *Anatomy of Film.* New York: St. Martin's Press, 1978, pp. 48–51. An interesting, brief discussion of thematic structure in the film.

Froug, William. "Ring Lardner, Jr." In *The Screenwriter Looks at the Screenwriter.* New York: Dell Publishing, 1972, pp. 115–41. A lengthy interview with Lardner about *M*A*S*H* authorship, and an examination of Lardner's background.

McCarthy, Todd. *"The Delinquents."* In *Kings of the Bs.* Edited by Todd McCarthy and Charles Flynn. New York: E. P. Dutton, 1975, pp. 215–19. A rare discussion of the production of the film, with an attempt to demonstrate its importance to Altman's career.

Monaco, James. "Robert Altman and the Myth of the Character." In *American Film Now*. New York: Oxford University Press, 1979, pp. 312–27. An interesting, "hip" treatment of Altman films to *A Wedding;* tries to demonstrate why elements other than characterization are important to the director.

Monaghan, Jay. "The Discovery of Buffalo Bill" and "The Wild West Show." In *The Great Rascal*. Boston: Little, Brown, 1951, pp. 3–33. A complete and accurate historical biography of Ned Buntline, his interactions with William Cody, and the genesis of the Buffalo Bill myth.

Plecki, Gerard. "The South in the Films of Robert Altman." In *The South and Film*. Edited by Warren French. Jackson: University Press of Mississippi, 1981, pp. 134–42. Discusses the South as a cross-section of American attitudes and life-styles as represented in four Altman films: *M*A*S*H, Brewster McCloud, Thieves Like Us,* and *Nashville*.

Wicking, Christopher, and **Vahimagi, Tise.** "Robert Altman." In *The American Vein*. New York: E. P. Dutton, 1979, pp. 85–86. A fairly complete listing of Altman's television experience, 1956–64.

3. Periodicals

Altman, Robert. "Interview." *Dialogue on Film*, February 1975, pp. 1–24. Altman speaking on production and technique in his films up to *Nashville*.

———. "Interview." *Post Script*, Fall 1981, pp. 2–7. A panel discussion after the screening of *Health* and *McCabe* in Baltimore, conducted and moderated by Leo Braudy and Robert Kolker.

Atlas, Jacoba, and **Guerin, Ann.** "Robert Altman, Julie Christie, and Warren Beatty Make the Western Real." *Show*, August 1971, pp. 18–21. Lengthy Altman interview and analysis on the problems of shooting and editing *McCabe*.

Baker, Charles A. "The Theme of Structure in the Films of Robert Altman." *Journal of Popular Film* 2 (Summer 1973):243–61. An examination of imagery and theme in Altman films up to *Images*.

Brackett, Leigh. "From *The Big Sleep* and *The Long Goodbye*." *Take One* 4 (January 1974):3–14. Describes how her previous collaboration on a Chandler adaptation influence the writing of the Altman version of *The Long Goodbye*.

Byrne, Connie, and **Lopez, William.** "*Nashville*." *Film Quarterly* 29, no. 2 (Winter 1975–76):13–25. An in-depth examination of *Nashville* production techniques, with interviews with Altman, Tewkesbury, and the film's editor, Sid Levin. Also includes an interview with Richard Baskin and a critical analysis.

Combs, Richard. "Playing the Game." *Sight and Sound*, Summer 1979, pp. 136–42. Details narrative and thematic problems in *Buffalo Bill*, with a commentary on the postproduction release struggle with the de Laurentiis organization.

Corliss, Richard. "Bisontennial Celebration." *New Times*, 23 July 1976, pp. 67–70. A criticism of *Buffalo Bill* and *Nashville* for being too pedantic; then (contradictorily) praises *Buffalo Bill* for its political and historical relevance and insight.

————. "This Isn't a Wedding, It's a Circus." *New Times*, 16 October 1978, pp. 74–78. Attacks *A Wedding* for its facile treatment of characters; compares the characterizations to the treatment (humiliation) of Major Burns in *M*A*S*H*.

Cutts, John. "*M*A*S*H, McCloud,* and *McCabe.*" *Films and Filming,* November 1971, pp. 40–48. A particularly informative interview with Altman on the making of three films.

Dawson, Jan. "Robert Altman Speaking." *Film Comment* March–April 1974, pp. 40–41. Altman describes how *The Long Goodbye* is a satire of films, not of Chandler. He is bidding farewell to Marlowe and to the genre.

Dempsey, Michael. "Altman: The Empty Staircase and the Chinese Princess." *Film Comment,* September-October 1974, pp. 10–17. Taking his title from the final scene in *Thieves* (in the train station) and the rumors about the prostitutes in *McCabe,* Dempsey describes the unconventional and "offbeat" nature of Altman's works, and explains why Altman seems interested in the mystique of film.

Engle, Gary. "*McCabe and Mrs. Miller.*" *Journal of Popular Film* 1 (Fall 1972):268–287. A sophisticated treatment of *McCabe* as an anti-Western; describes the aspects of the genre Altman subverts.

Fox, Terry Curtis. "*Nashville Chats.*" *Chicago Reader,* 4 July 1976, pp. 1–20. A very lengthy, detailed interview with Altman in which he talks about the songs, writing, and shooting of *Nashville.* Very candid, interesting remarks on *California Split* and *Buffalo Bill* as well.

Gregory, Charles. "Knight Without Meaning." *Sight and Sound,* Summer 1973, pp. 155–59. A review of Philip Marlowe in films; argues that Altman's Marlowe is inconsistent with previous Marlowes and, ultimately, unsubstantial.

Harmetz, Aljean. "The 15th Man Who Was Asked to Direct *M*A*S*H* (And Did) Makes a Peculiar Western." *New York Times Magazine,* 20 June 1971, pp. 11–54. Explains at length many aspects of *McCabe's* production. Interviews with Beatty and Christie on the set are given, along with comments on Altman's television and film background.

Jameson, Richard T. "*Nashville.*" *Movietown News,*" 4 September 1957, pp. 2–8. A good treatment of Nashville in which Altman describes why "writing it down kinda makes me feel better."

Johnson, David. "Images." *Show,* October 1972, pp. 47–50. Altman comments on his intentions for characterization in the film, describing his complex idea for each person's problem.

Kinder, Marsha. "The Art of Dreaming in *Three Women* and *Providence.*" *Film Quarterly* 31 no. 1 (Fall 1977):10–18. A discussion of the "highly condensed visual dream" of *Three Women* from which the narrative grows.

————. "The Return of the Outlaw Couple." *Film Quarterly* 27, no. 4 (Summer 1974): 2–10. Differentiates between *Thieves* and *Bonnie and Clyde* because the "outlaws" in *Thieves* are naive, not rebellious. Compares the film to Malick's *Badlands* in terms of cinematography, characterizations, and themes.

Kovacs, Lazlo, and Zsigmond, Vilmos. "Interview." *Dialogue on Film* October 1974, pp. 1–28. The two cinematographers describe working with Altman in detail on films up to *The Long Goodbye*, with special attention paid to *Images.*

Levine, Robert. "Robert Altman and Company." *Film Comment*, January-February 1977, pp. 4–13. Discusses Altman, Rudolph, and Benton, with a lengthy interview with Benton on Altman as *The Late Show* producer (entitled "Marlowe in Nighttown").

Lipnick, Edward. "The Long Goodbye." *American Cinematographer* 54 (March 1975):278–81. A technical description of the "creative post-flashing" processing of the film.

Macklin, F. Anthony. "Welcome to Lion's Gate." *Film Heritage*, Fall 1976, pp. 1–17. An interview with Alan Rudolph and Richard Baskin, describing the writing of *Buffalo Bill*, the shooting of *California Split* and *Nashville*, and an evaluation of the "mixed" quality of *Nashville* songs.

Michener, Charles, and **Kasindorf, Martin.** "Epic of Opryland." *Newsweek*, 30 June 1975, pp. 46–50. A description of the *Nashville* production, in which Altman comments that "casting is 90% of the creation."

Milne, Tom. "*California Split.*" *Sight and Sound*, Winter 1974–75, pp. 55–56. The thesis is that the film is about freedom of choice and chance. Argues that the film's structure is based on the relationship between Charlie and Bill, and on the omnipresence of obsession.

Monaco, James. "Welcome to Palm Springs." *Literature/Film Quarterly* 6 (Spring 1978): 15–25. Describes the setting and theme of *Three Women* and compares it to Rudolph's *Welcome to L.A.*

Moyer, Kermit. "Did You Ever See an Elephant Fly?" *Film Heritage*, Fall 1975, pp. 12–16. An examination of style and "substance" in Altman films; based on the metaphorical riddle in *California Split*.

Oliver, Bill. "*The Long Goodbye* and *Chinatown.*" *Literature/Film Quarterly* 3 (Summer 1975): 240–48. A topical discussion of how the two films challenged the private-eye tradition.

Reid, Max. "The Making of *California Split.*" *Filmmakers Newsletter*, October 1974, pp. 24–27. An interview with Altman on the shooting of the film; complete background information on sound recording in that film.

Rosenbaum, Jonathan. "Improvisations and Interactions in Altmanville." *Sight and Sound*, Spring 1975, pp. 90–95. An excellent examination of the use of "improvised" dialogue in *California Split* and *McCabe:* an analysis also of the use of the title song (melody and lyrics) in *The Long Goodbye.*

———. "*Nashville.*" *Sight and Sound*, Autumn 1975, pp. 254–55. Argues that the film leaps from an exciting production process and a stimulating unraveling of the narrative "into the limited vocabulary and closed circuits of a public forum."

———. "*A Wedding:* An Altman." *Film Comment*, September-October 1978, pp. 12–18. Examines the implication he draws from several films, that "Altman has something important to say, even though he can't quite believe it and isn't quite sure what it is."

Sarris, Andrew. "Bottom Line Buffaloes Altman." *Village Voice*, 5 July 1976, pp. 107–9. Describes that what is lacking from *Buffalo* is any affection for the subject; relates the distribution fracas with de Laurentiis.

———. "New Pillars of the Pantheon." *Village Voice*, 3 July 1978, pp. 39–40. Places Altman in a group of "dissonant directors" who approach "pantheon" auteur status.

Self, Robert. "Invention and Death: The Commodities of Media in *Nashville*." *Journal of Popular Film* 5 (1976):2–20. A sociological and popular-culture perspective on the theme of media involvement with politics in *Nashville;* the analysis of John Triplette is problematic.

Stewart, Garrett. "*The Long Goodbye* from *Chinatown*," *Film Quarterly* 28, no. 2 (Winter 1974–75):25–32. Argues that *Chinatown* draws directly from Altman's inventions for Marlowe and that *The Long Goodbye* was "the masterwork of America's most interesting working director."

"**Stormy Saga of *Popeye*.**" *American Film*, December 1980, pp. 30–36, 73–74. An excellent description of the beginning of the *Popeye* project, the casting, the interaction among crew members, and lengthy comments of Altman and Feiffer. An accurate and detailed account of the problems, conflicts, and cooperation that abounded on the project.

Tarantino, Michael. "Movement as Metaphor: *The Long Goodbye*." *Sight and Sound*, Spring 1975, pp. 91–102. Examines camera movement in eight specific scenes in the film, arguing that movement establishes a "deterministic atmosphere which pervades the film."

Tewkesbury, Joan. "Dialogue on Film." *American Film*, March 1979, pp. 35–46. Describes her collaborations with Altman and his experimental sensibility. Relates details of the generation of the political subtext in *Nashville*.

Williams, Alan. "*California Split*." *Film Quarterly* 28 no. 3 (Spring 1975):54–55. A brief, brilliant commentary on the conflicts within the film. Describes the film as "a tale of coming apart," which has as its subject "emptiness." Examines how the director "works through a rambling narrative in a disciplined way."

4. Unpublished Material

Altman, Robert. *Images* (1966). Factor-Altman-Mirell Films Ltd., Los Angeles, California. 127 pp. First draft by Altman following his thirty pages of handwritten and typed notes.

———. *The Presbyterian Church Wager.* David Foster Productions, dated 19 January 1971. 122 pp. Altman's adaption of the novel *McCabe* by Edmund Naughton. Provides examples of the types of reductive changes that occurred from script to screen.

———. Interview for Cinema Arts Series, no. 13152. New York, 1978, 60 minutes. Altman describes at length the typical stages of filmmaking for himself, and compares it to traditional Hollywood procedure.

Feiffer, Jules. "Popeye." Los Angeles: Paramount Pictures, 1979. Duplicated by Paramount Print Shop. 145 pp. The final draft of the Feiffer script, based on the E. C. Segar comic strip. Illustrates how drastically the original order of scenes and the dialogue were changed in the shooting.

Tewkesbury, Joan. "Thieves Like Us." Lion's Gate Films, 1973. 122 pp. The Tewkesbury adaptation based on the Edward Anderson novel. Most useful when compared to the novel, this script also provides details of characterization about Bowie and T-Dub (i.e., superstitious natures) not immediately evident in the film.

Filmography

THE DELINQUENTS (Imperial Productions/United Artists, 1957)
Producer: Robert Altman
Assistant Director: Reza Badiyi
Screenplay: Robert Altman
Cinematographer: Charles Paddock
Art Director: Chet Allen
Production Manager: Joan Altman
Music: Bill Nolan Quintet Minus Two
Sound: Bob Post
Sound Effects: Fred Brown
Editor: Helene Turner
Cast: Tom Laughlin (Scotty), Peter Miller (Cholly), Richard Bakalyn (Eddy),
Rosemary Howard (Janice), Helene Hawley (Mrs. White), Lotus Corelli (Mrs.
Wilson), Christine Altman (Sissy)
Running Time: 72 minutes

THE JAMES DEAN STORY (Warner Brothers, 1957)
Producer: Robert Altman and George W. George
Assistant Producer: Lou Lombardo
Co-director: George W. George
Screenplay: Stewart Stern
Cinematographer: Thirty various cameramen
Production Designer: Louis Clyde Stoumen
Music: Leith Stevens
Sound: Cathey Burrow
Editors: Robert Altman and George W. George
Narration: Martin Gabel
Cast: Marcus, Ortense, and Markie Winslow (Dean's aunt, uncle, and cousin),
Mr. and Mrs. Dean (Dean's grandparents), Adeline Hall (drama teacher), Jerry
Luce, Louis de Liso, Arnie Langer, Arline Sax, Officer Nelson (highway
patrolman)
Running Time: 83 minutes

NIGHTMARE IN CHICAGO (Roncom/Universal, 1964)
Producer: Robert Altman

Screenplay: Donald Moessinger, from William P. McGivern's novel *Death on the Turnpike*
Cinematographer: Bud Thackery
Music: John Williams
Cast: Charles McGraw (Georgie Porgie), Ted Knight (reporter), Robert Ridgely, Philip Abbott, Barbara Turner, John Alonzo, Charlene Lee
Running Time: 81 minutes

COUNTDOWN (Warner Brothers, 1968)
Executive Producer: William Conrad
Assistant Director: Victor Vallejo
Screenplay: Loring Mandel, from Hank Searls's novel *The Pilgrim Project*
Cinematographer: William W. Spencer
Art Director: Jack Poplin
Set decoration: Ralph S. Hurst
Music: Leonard Rosenman
Sound: Everett A. Hughes
Editor: Gene Milford
Cast: James Caan (Lee), Robert Duvall (Chiz), Joanna Moore (Mickey), Charles Aidman (Guss), Steve Ihnat (Ross), Michael Murphy (Rick), Ted Knight (Larson)
Running Time: 101 minutes

THAT COLD DAY IN THE PARK (Factor-Altman-Mirell Films)
Commonwealth United Entertainment, Inc., 1969)
Producers: Donald Factor and Leon Mirell
Associate Producer: Robert Eggenweiler
Assistant Director: Harold Schneider
Screenplay: Gillian Freeman, From Gerald Perrau Saussine's novel
Cinematographer: Lazlo Kovacs
Art Director: Leon Eickson
Production Manager: James Margellos
Music: Johnny Mandel
Sound: John Gusselle
Editor: Danford Green
Cast: Sandy Dennis (Frances Austen), Michael Burns (the young man), Suzanne Benton (Nina), Luana Anders (Sylvie), Michael Murphy (the Rounder)
Running Time: 112 minutes

M*A*S*H (Aspen/Twentieth Century–Fox, 1970)
Producer: Ingo Preminger
Associate Producer: Leon Erickson
Assistant Director: Ray Taylor, Jr.
Screenplay: Ring Lardner, Jr., from Richard Hooker's novel
Cinematographer: Harold E. Stine
Art Directors: Jack Martin Smith and Arthur Lonergan
Set Decoration: Walter M. Scott and Start A. Reiss
Music: Johnny Mandel (song "Suicide Is Painless," lyrics by Mike Altman)
Sound: Bernard Freericks and John Stack

Editor: Danford B. Greene
Cast: Donald Sutherland (Hawkeye Pierce), Elliott Gould (Trapper John
McIntyre), Tom Skerritt (Duke Forrest), Sally Kellerman (Major Hot Lips),
Robert Duvall (Major Frank Burns), Jo Ann Pflug (Lt. Dish), René Auberjonois
(Dago Red), Roger Bowen (Col. Henry Blake), Gary Burghoff (Radar O'Reilly),
David Arkin (Sgt. Major Vollmer), Fred Williamson (Spearchucker), Michael
Murphy (Me Lay), Kim Atwood (Ho-Jon), Tim Brown (Corporal Judson), John
Schuck (Painless Pole), G. Wood (General Hammond), Bud Cort (Private
Boone), Corey Fischer (Capt. Bandini)
Running Time: 116 minutes

BREWSTER McCLOUD (Adler-Philips/Lion's Gate for M-G-M, 1970)
Producer: Lou Adler
Associate Producers: Robert Eggenweiler and James Margellos
Assistant Director: Tommy Thompson
Screenplay: Brian McKay (uncredited), William Doran Cannon from his short
story
Cinematographers: Jordan Cronenweth and Lamar Boren
Art Director: George W. Davis and Preston Ames
Music: Gene Page
Sound: Harry W. Tetrick and William McCaughey
Editor: Lou Lombardo
Cast: Bud Cort (Brewster McCloud), Sally Kellerman (Louise), Michael Murphy
(Frank Shaft), William Windom (Haskel Weeks), Shelley Duvall (Suzanne Davis),
René Auberjonois (lecturer), Stacy Keach (Abraham Wright), John Schuck (Lt.
Alvin Johnson), Margaret Hamilton (Daphne Heap), Jennifer Salt (Hope), Corey
Fischer (Lt. Hines), G. Wood (Capt. Crandall), Bert Remsen (Douglas Breen),
Angelin Johnson (Mrs. Breen), Ellis Gilbert (butler), Verdie Henshaw (Feathered
Nest Sanatorium manager)
Running Time: 105 minutes

McCABE AND MRS. MILLER (Warner Brothers, 1971)
Producers: David Foster and Mitchell Brower
Associate Producer: Robert Eggenweiler
Assistant Director: Tommy Thompson
Screenplay: Robert Altman, Brian McKay, from Edmund Naughton's novel
McCabe
Cinematographer: Vilmos Zsigmond
Art Directors: Philip Thomas and Al Locatelli
Production Designer: Leon Erickson
Music: Leonard Cohen
Sound: John V. Gusselle and William A. Thompson
Editor: Louis Lombardo
Cast: Warren Beatty (John McCabe), Julie Christie (Constance Miller), René
Auberjonois (Sheehan), Hugh Millais (Dog Butler), Shelley Duvall (Ida Coyle),
Michael Murphy (Sears), John Schuck (Smalley), Corey Fischer (Mr. Elliott)
Running Time: 121 minutes

IMAGES (Lion's Gate Films/The Hemdale Group/Columbia Pictures, 1972)
Producer: Tommy Thompson
Assistant Director: Seamus Byrne
Screenplay: Robert Altman (with passages from Susannah York's *In Search of Unicorns*)
Cinematographer: Vilmos Zsigmond
Art Director: Leon Erickson
Music: John Williams
Sound: Liam Saurin, Stomu Yamashta, Rodney Holland
Editor: Graeme Clifford
Cast: Susannah York (Cathryn), René Auberjonois (Hugh), Hugh Millais (Marcel), Marcel Bozzuffi (René), Cathryn Harrison (Susannah)
Running Time: 101 minutes

THE LONG GOODBYE (Lion's Gate Films/United Artists, 1973)
Producer: Jerry Bick
Executive Producer: Elliot Kastner
Associate Producer: Robert Eggenweiler
Assistant Directors: Tommy Thompson and Alan Rudolph
Screenplay: Leigh Brackett, from Raymond Chandler's novel
Cinematographer: Vilmos Zsigmond
Music: John Williams (song "The Long Goodbye" by Johnny Mercer and John Williams)
Editor: Lou Lombardo
Cast: Elliott Gould (Philip Marlowe), Nina van Pallandt (Eileen Wade), Sterling Hayden (Roger Wade), Mark Rydell (Marty Augustine), Henry Gibson (Dr. Verringer), David Arkin (Harry), Jim Bouton (Terry Lennox), Jo Ann Brody (Jo Ann Eggenweiler)
Running Time: 111 minutes

THIEVES LIKE US (United Artists, 1974)
Executive Producer: George Litto
Producer: Jerry Bick
Associate Producers: Robert Eggenweiler and Thomas Hal Philips
Assistant Director: Tommy Thompson
Screenplay: Calder Willingham, Joan Tewkesbury, Robert Altman from Edward Anderson's novel
Cinematographer: Jean Boffety
Visual Consultants: Jack DeGovia and Scott Bushnell
Sound: Don Matthews
Editor: Lou Lombardo
Cast: Keith Carradine (Bowie Bowers), Shelley Duvall (Keechie), John Schuck (Chicamaw), Bert Remsen (T-Dub), Louise Fletcher (Mattie), Ann Latham (Lula), Tom Skerritt (Dee Mobley), Joan Tewkesbury (lady in train station)
Running Time: 123 minutes

CALIFORNIA SPLIT (Won World/Persky Bright/Reno for Columbia Pictures, 1974)

Producer: Robert Altman and Joseph Walsh
Executive Producers: Aaron Spelling and Leonard Goldberg
Associate Producer: Robert Eggenweiler
Assistant Director: Tommy Thompson
Screenplay: Joseph Walsh
Cinematographer: Paul Lohmann
Art Director: Leon Erickson
Sound: Jim Webb and Kay Rose
Editor: Lou Lombardo
Cast: Elliott Gould (Charlie Waters), George Segal (Bill Denny), Ann Prentiss (Barbara Miller), Gwen Welles (Susan Peters), Edward Walsh (Lew), Joseph Walsh (Sparkie), Bert Remsen ("Helen Brown"), Jeff Goldblum (Lloyd Harris), Jack Riley (second bartender), "Amarillo Slim" Preston, Winston Lee, Harry Drackett, Thomas Hal Phillips, Ted Say, A. J. Hood (Reno poker players)
Running Time: 109 minutes

NASHVILLE (ABC Entertainment/Paramount Pictures, 1975)
Producer: Robert Altman
Executive Producers: Martin Starger and Jerry Weintraub
Associate Producers: Robert Eggenweiler and Scott Bushnell
Assistant Directors: Tommy Thompson and Alan Rudolph
Screenplay: Joan Tewkesbury
Cinematographer: Paul Lohmann
Music: Richard Baskin
Songs: "200 Years" (lyrics by Henry Gibson, music by Richard Baskin), "Let Me Be the One" (lyrics and music by Richard Baskin), "Bluebird" (lyrics and music by Ronee Blakley), "Memphis" (lyrics and music by Karen Black), "For the Sake of the Children" (lyrics and music by Richard Baskin and Richard Reicheg), "Keep a' Goin" (lyrics by Henry Gibson, music by Richard Baskin and Henry Gibson), "Rolling Stone" (lyrics and music by Karen Black), "Tapedeck in His Tractor (The Cowboy Song)" (lyrics and music by Ronee Blakley), "I Never Get Enough" (lyrics and music by Richard Baskin and Ben Raleith), "One, I Love You" (lyrics and music by Richard Baskin), "I'm Easy" (lyrics and music by Keith Carradine), "It Don't Worry Me" (lyrics and music by Keith Carradine), "My Idaho Home" (lyrics and music by Ronee Blakley)
Sound: Jim Webb and Chris McLaughlin
Editor: Sidney Levin and Dennis Hill
Cast: David Arkin (Norman), Barbara Baxley (Lady Pearl), Ned Beatty (Delbert Reese), Karen Black (Connie White), Ronee Blakley (Barbara Jean), Timothy Brown (Tommy Brown), Keith Carradine (Tom Frank), Geraldine Chaplin (Opal), Robert Doqui (Wade), Shelley Duvall (L.A. Joan), Allen Garfield (Barnett), Henry Gibson (Haven Hamilton), Scott Glenn (Pfc. Glenn Kelly), Jeff Goldblum (Tricycle Man), Barbara Harris (Albuquerque), David Hayward (Kenny Fraiser), Michael Murphy (John Triplette), Allan Nicholls (Bill), Dave Peel (Bud Hamilton), Cristina Raines (Mary), Bert Remsen (Star), Lily Tomlin (Linnea Reese), Gwen Welles (Sueleen Gay), Keenan Wynn (Mr. Green), Richard Baskin (Frog), Elliott Gould and Julie Christie (themselves)
Running Time: 159 minutes

BUFFALO BILL AND THE INDIANS, OR, SITTING BULL'S HISTORY LESSON (Dino de Laurentiis Corporation/Lion's Gate Films/Talent Associates Norton Simon/United Artists, 1976)
Producer: Robert Altman
Executive Producer: David Susskind
Associate Producers: Robert Eggenweiler, Scott Bushnell, and Jack Cashin
Assistant Director: Tommy Thompson
Screenplay: Alan Rudolph and Robert Altman, based on Arthur Kopit's play *Indians*
Cinematographer: Paul Lohmann
Art Director: Jack Maxsted
Set Decorations: Denny Parrish
Costumes: Allen Highfill
Music: Richard Baskin
Sound: Jim Webb and Chris McLaughlin
Editors: Peter Appleton and Dennis Hill
Cast: Paul Newman (the Star), Joel Grey (the Producer), Kevin McCarthy (the Publicist), Harvey Keitel (the Relative), Allan Nicholls (the Journalist), Geraldine Chaplin (the Sure Shot), John Considine (the Sure Shot's Manager), Robert Doqui (the Wrangler), Bert Remsen (the Bartender), Denver Pyle (the Indian Agent), Frank Kaquitts (the Indian), Will Sampson (the Interpreter), Fred N. Larsen (the King of the Cowboys), Humphrey Gratz (the Old Soldier), Pat McCormick (the President of the United States), Shelley Duvall (the First Lady), Burt Lancaster (the Legend Maker)
Running Time: 118 minutes

THREE WOMEN (Lion's Gate Films/Twentieth Century–Fox, 1977)
Producer: Robert Altman
Screenplay: Robert Altman
Cinematographer: Chuck Rosher
Art Director: James D. Vance
Set Decoration: Patricia Resnick
Music: Gerald Busby
Sound: Jim Webb and Chris McLaughlin
Editor: Dennis Hill
Cast: Shelley Duvall (Millie Lammoreaux), Sissy Spacek (Pinky Rose), Janice Rule (Willie Hart), Robert Fortier (Edgar Hart), Ruth Nelson (Mrs. Rose), John Cromwell (Mr. Rose)
Running Time: 124 minutes

A WEDDING (Lion's Gate Films/Twentieth Century–Fox, 1978)
Producer: Robert Altman
Executive Producer: Tommy Thompson
Associate Producers: Robert Eggenweiler and Scott Bushnell
Assistant Director: Tommy Thompson
Screenplay: John Considine, Patricia Resnick, Allan Nicholls, and Robert Altman based on a story by Robert Altman and John Considine
Cinematographer: Charles Rosher

Sound: Jim Webb, Chris McLaughlin, and Jim Stuebe
Editor: Tony Lombardo
Cast: The Groom's Family: Lillian Gish (Nettie Sloan), Ruth Nelson (Beatrice
Sloan Cory), Desi Arnaz, Jr. (Dino Corelli, the groom), Vittorio Gassman (Luigi
Corelli), Nina Van Pallandt (Regina Corelli), Dina Merrill (Antoinette Sloan
Goddard), Pat McCormick (Mackenzie Goddard). The Brides Family: Carol
Burnett (Tulip Brenner), Paul Dooley (Snooks Brenner), Amy Stryker (Muffin
Brenner, the bride), Mia Farrow (Buffy Brenner), Dennis Christopher (Hughie
Brenner). The Staff: Cedric Scott (Randolph), Robert Fortier (Jim Habor,
gardener), Maureen Steindler (Libby Clinton, cook), Geraldine Chaplin (Rita
Billingsley), Viveca Lindfors (Ingrid Hellstrom), Lauren Hutton (Flo Farmer),
Allan Nicholls (Jake Jacobs), John Considine (Jeff Kuykendall), Patricia Resnick
(Redford), Dennis Franz (Koons). The Friends: Howard Duff (Dr. Jules
Meecham), John Cromwell (Bishop Martin), Bert Remsen (William Williamson)
Running Time: 124 minutes

QUINTET (Lion's Gate Film/Twentieth Century–Fox, 1979)
Producer: Robert Altman
Executive Producer: Tommy Thompson
Assistant Director: Tommy Thompson
Screenplay: Frank Barhydt, Robert Altman, and Patricia Resnick, from a story by
Robert Altman, Patricia Resnick, and Lionel Chetwynd
Cinematographer: Jean Boffety
Production Design: Leon Erickson
Costumes: Scott Bushnell
Music: Tom Pierson
Editor: Dennis Hill
Cast: Paul Newman (Essex), Bibi Andersson (Ambrosia), Bridgette Fossey (Vivia),
Fernando Rey (Grigor), Vittorio Gassman (St. Christopher), Nina Van Pallandt
(Deuca), David Langton (Redstone), Craig Nelson (Goldstar), Tom Hill (Francha)
Running Time: 110 minutes

A PERFECT COUPLE (Lion's Gate Films/Twentieth Century–Fox, 1979)
Producer: Robert Altman
Executive Producer: Tommy Thompson
Associate Producers: Robert Eggenweiler and Scott Bushnell
Assistant Director: Tommy Thompson
Screenplay: Robert Altman and Allan Nicholls
Set Decoration: Leon Erickson
Music: Allan Nicholls
Sound: Robert Gravenor
Editor: Tony Lombardo
Cast: Paul Dooley (Alex Theodopoulos), Marta Heflin (Sheila Shea), Titos Vandis
(Alex's Father), Belito Moreno (Eleausa), Henry Gibson (Fred Batt), Dimitra
Arliss (Athena), Allan Nicholls (Dana 115), Ann Ryerson (Skye 147), Dennis
Franz (Costa), Margery Bond (Wilma), Ted Neeley (Teddy)
Running Time: 110 minutes

HEALTH (Lion's Gate Films/Twentieth Century–Fox, 1980)
Producer: Robert Altman
Executive Producer: Tommy Thompson
Associate Producers: Scott Bushnell, Wolf Kroeger
Assistant Director: Tommy Thompson
Screenplay: Robert Altman, Frank Barhydt, Paul Dooley
Cinematographer: Edmond L. Koons
Art Director: Robert Quinn
Production Manager: Robert Eggenweiler
Sound: Robert Gravenor and Don Merritt
Editors: Dennis Hill and Tom Benko
Cast: Carol Burnett (Gloria Burbank), Lauren Bacall (Esther Brill), James Garner
(Harry Wolff), Glenda Jackson (Isabella Garnell), Diane Stilwell (Willow Wertz),
Henry Gibson (Bobby Hammer), Paul Dooley (Dr. Gill Gainey), Donald Moffat
(Col. Cody), Alfre Woodard (Sally Benbow), Ann Ryerson (Dr. Ruth Ann Jackie),
Robert Fortier (Chief of Security), Allan Nicholls (Jake Jacobs), MacIntyre Dixon
(Fred Munson), Dick Cavett and Dinah Shore (themselves)
Running Time: 96 minutes

POPEYE (Paramount Pictures/Walt Disney Productions, 1980)
Producer: Robert Evans
Executive Producer: C. O. Erickson
Associate Producer: Scott Bushnell
Assistant Directors: Bob Dahlin and Victor Tourjansky
Screenplay: Jules Feiffer, based on E. C. Segar's "Popeye" characters
Cinematographer: Giuseppe Rotunno
Production Design: Wolf Kroeger
Location Manager: Robert Eggenweiler
Costumes: Scott Bushnell
Music and Lyrics: Harry Nilsson (additional score by Tom Pierson)
Sound: Robert Gravenor
Sound Effects: Teresa Eckton and Andy Patterson
Editors: John W. Holmes and Davie Simmons
Supervising Editor: Tony Lombardo
Cast: Robin Williams (Popeye), Shelley Duvall (Olive Oyl), Ray Walston
(Poopdeck Pappy), Paul Dooley (Wimpy), Paul L. Smith (Bluto), Richard
Libertini (Geezil), Donald Moffat (The Taxman), MacIntyre Dixon (Cole Oyl),
Roberta Maxwell (Nana Oyl), Donovan Scott (Caster Oyl), Allan Nicholls (Rough
House), Wesley Ivan Hurt (Swee' Pea), Bill Irwin (Ham Gravy, the Old
Boyfriend), Robert Fortier (Bill Barnacle, The Town Drunk), Linda Hunt (Mrs.
Oxheart), Carlo Pellegrini (Swifty, The Cook), Dennis Franz (Spike), David Arkin
(The Mailman/Policeman)
Running Time: 111 minutes

COME BACK TO THE FIVE AND DIME, JIMMY DEAN, JIMMY DEAN
(Sandcastle 5 Productions/Mark Goodson Presentation/Viacom Enterprises/
Cinecom International Films, 1982)

Producer: Scott Bushnell
Executive Producer: Giraud Chester
Assistant Director: Sonja Webster
Screenplay: Ed Graczyk, based on his play
Cinematographer: Pierre Mignot
Production Design: David Cropman
Production Executive: Peter Newman
Production Manager: Sonja Webster
Production Coordinator: Doug Cole
Costumes: Scott Bushnell
Music: Allan Nicholls
Editor: Jason Rosenfield
Cast: Sandy Dennis (Mona), Cher (Sissy), Karen Black (Joanne), Sudie Bond
(Juanita), Marta Heflin (Edna Louise), Kathy Bates (Stella Mae), Mark Patton
(Joe)
Running Time: 102 minutes
Originally produced on Broadway by Dan Fisher, Joseph Clapsaddle, Joel
Brykman, and Jack Lawrence

STREAMERS (Mileti Prod/United Artists Classics, 1983)
Producers: Robert Altman and Nick J. Mileti
Executive Producers: Robert Michael Geiser and John Roberdeau
Associate Producer: Scott Bushnell
Assistant Director: Allan Nicholls
Screenplay: David Rabe, from his play
Cinematographer: Pierre Mignot
Art Director: Steve Altman
Set Decoration: Robert Brown
Set Design: Wolf Kroeger
Costumes: Scott Bushnell
Editor: Norman C. Smith
Cast: Mitchell Lichenstein (Richie), Matthew Modine (Billy), David Alan Grier
(Roger), Michael Wright (Carlyle), Guy Boyd (Rooney), George Dzundza
(Cokes), Albert Macklin (Martin)
Running Time: 118 minutes
Distributed in 16mm by United Artists Classics

Additional Productions for Lion's Gate Films

1977   **WELCOME TO L.A.**   Directed by Alan Rudolph
                             Produced by Robert Altman
1977   **THE LATE SHOW**   Directed by Robert Benton
                           Produced by Robert Altman
1978   **REMEMBER MY NAME**   Directed by Alan Rudolph
                              Produced by Robert Altman

1979 **RICH KIDS** Directed by Robert Young
Produced by Robert Altman

Television Directing Credits

1956 **THE MILLIONARE**

1957 **ALFRED HITCHCOCK PRESENTS:** "The Young One,"
"Together"
WHIRLYBIRDS: "The Midnight Show," "A Matter of Trust,"
"Guilty of Old Age," "Christmas in June"

1958 **WHIRLYBIRDS:** "Till Death Do Us Part," "Time Limit,"
"Experiment X-74," "The Big Lie," "The Perfect Crime," "The
Unknown Soldier," "Two of a Kind," "In Ways Mysterious," "The
Black Maria," "The Sitting"

1959 **HAWAIIAN EYE:** "Three Tickets to Lani"
LAWMAN: "The Robbery"
SHERIFF OF COCHISE
THE DETECTIVES
THE TROUBLESHOOTERS

1960 **SURFSIDE SIX:** "Thieves Among Honor"
SUGARFOOT: "Apollo With a Gun," "The Highbinder"
BRONCO: "The Mustangers"
ROARING TWENTIES: "The Prairie Flower," "Brother's Keeper,"
"White Carnation," "Dance Marathon"
MAVERICK: "Bolt from the Blue."
BONANZA (Produced for NBC by David Dortort; Associate
Producer: Tommy Thompson; Assistant Directors: John E. Burch
and Ralph E. Black; Unit Manager: Andrew Durkus; Series II):
"Silent Thunder" (Script: John Furia, Jr. Production no. 30713.
Aired October 20, 1960). "Bank Run" (Script: N. B. Stone, Jr.
Production no. 30719. Aired November 17, 1960)

1961 **BONANZA:** "The Duke" (Script: William R. Cox. Production no.
30725. Aired January 31, 1961) "The Mustang" (Formerly "Sam
Hill." Script: not available. Production no. 30730. Aired February 7,
1961) "The Rival" (Formerly "The Witness." Script: Anthony
Lawrence. Production no. 30728. Aired March 6, 1961) "The
Secret" (Script: Jack Hawkins. Production no. 30732. Aired March
13, 1961) "The Dream Riders" (Script: Jack McCan and James Von
Wagoner. Production no. 30734. Aired March 27, 1961) "The Many
Faces of Gideon Finch" (Script: Vincent Wright. Production no.
31251. Aired August 21, 1961)
ROARING TWENTIES: "Two a Day," "Right off the Boat" (two
parts), "Royal Tour," "Standing Room Only"
HAWAIIAN EYE: "Touch of Larceny"
M SQUAD: "Lovers' Lane Killing"
DESILU MYSTERY THEATER: "Death of a Dream"

ROUTE 66: "Some of the People Some of the Time"
BUS STOP: "Country General," "The Covering Darkness," "Door Without a Key," "Summer Lightning," "Pursuit of Evil"

1962   THE GALLANT MEN (pilot)
        THE LONG HOT SUMMER (pilot)
        EAST SIDE, WEST SIDE

1963   KRAFT SUSPENSE THEATER: "The Long, Lost Life of Edward Smalley"
        COMBAT

1964   KRAFT SUSPENSE THEATER: "Once Upon a Savage Night"

16mm Rental Information

The following films are available in 16mm from Films Incorporated, 733 Green Bay Road, Wilmette, Il 60091:
THAT COLD DAY IN THE PARK
M*A*S*H
CALIFORNIA SPLIT
NASHVILLE
THREE WOMEN
A WEDDING
QUINTET
A PERFECT COUPLE
HEALTH
POPEYE
COMEBACK TO THE FIVE AND DIME, JIMMY DEAN, JIMMY DEAN

The following films are available from United Artists 16, 729 Seventh Avenue, New York, NY 10019:
THE LONG GOODBYE
THIEVES LIKE US
BUFFALO BILL AND THE INDIANS
STREAMERS

The following films are available from Warner Brothers Non-Theatrical Division, 4000 Warner Blvd., Burbank, CA 63166;
COUNTDOWN
BREWSTER McCLOUD
McCABE AND MRS. MILLER

Not available: THE DELINQUENTS and THE JAMES DEAN STORY

Index